Ancient Wisdom and Modern Science that Fuels Your Prime Capabilities

JOEL PUTHOFF

Have you ever wondered your abilities' extent in life? Have you ever desired a life where you can accomplish your desired goals with your highest-performing self?

By taking your wondering to a conscious level, you will begin to explore and cultivate habits designed to propel you forward with increased abilities and optimal momentum. How would you like to power through the challenges throughout this journey?

Capability Fuel takes a holistic approach to ancient wisdom and modern sciences that fuel an individual for sustainable and optimal performance. The further you push yourself outside the comfort zone to fulfill your most intentional goals, the more necessary it is to implement a set of habits and routines that help you accomplish these endeavors.

You can focus on many capabilities to achieve the desired progress, but only a core group of capabilities has the most consistent and transformable impact. Meanwhile, you will understand your capabilities' extent and learn to move beyond their limits by learning how to fuel their current components most effectively.

Are you ready to activate the fuels for propelling your most capable self forward?

TABLE OF CONTENTS

INTRODUCTION

1. Increase your "best-performing" days.
2. Engage your untapped potential and transcend beyond gaps.
3. Find out what you need for personal, physical, mental, and social development. Understand the unique fuels required for your situation.
4. Success, performance, and desire bypass ego and pride when filtered appropriately and stimulate authentic confidence.
5. The position of your focus determines your ability to capitalize your objectives. Dedication in one area can affect other vital aspects of your life that were once neglected.
6. The subconscious works both for us and against us.
7. Self-awareness check: How well do we really know our inner systems and capabilities?
8. Understand why we make the choices we do. We tend to feed off what we're good at instead of exploring what we could excel in.

9. Combine fuels for optimized strength.
10. Think in the way our wisest self would want us to think.
11. Progresses are more than black and white. Reality - Expectations = Level of Happiness. What matters is how we view our progress and who we eventually become.
12. Finding comfort in discomfort. Novel challenges are key to neuroplasticity.
13. Shift your winning gears. Adapt and adjust your growth focal points.
14. Respond effectively to damages to your mentality, physique, spirituality, and social sphere to avoid unprecedented setbacks.
15. Those who excel tend to have a quieter brain, whereas amateurs are "on fire" because the brain forms new connections while the amateur learns and grows.

CHAPTER 1

CHASING YOUR MOST CAPABLE SELF

"If we did all the things we were capable of, we would literally astound ourselves."

- Thomas A. Edison

There are three things I believe about you. First, I believe you are currently on a personal journey in which you are trying to capture your most capable self in the hopes of maximizing your life experiences. Second, I believe you are looking for additional knowledge and awareness of how to create optimal momentum for these life experiences you desire. Third, I believe you are already well on your way because you are taking necessary actions like grabbing this book to continue your pursuit to manifest and maximize your ideal journey.

Imagine how your life would change if you could perform at 90%-100% of your potential for the next two or three years. That is, achieving peak performance on almost every day for the next few years. Where could it take you? What experiences could you create for yourself?

Take a second to recall the most productive and fulfilling day of your life in your mind. Can you remember where you were, what you did, and how others responded to you? Most importantly, do you remember how confident and certain you felt about your personal or professional capabilities?

What if you could have more days like this on a more regular basis? Better yet, what if you could perform at this level 80% of your days?

Imagine where that would take you in just a few years. This book was written to help you accomplish that level of performance. Is this an impractical promise? The answer lies in you.

We are both aware that you've already experienced at least one high performance day. Some may have several a year, but only peak performers can live these days consistently.

I'm sure we can all agree that the most difficult part of the journey is the self-discipline that keeps you steadily on track. There are days when motivation disappears and the chemical complexities taking place within us, leave us drained and uninspired to push for more. This is when we need our fuels the most, to propel us through those challenging times and keep us determined for more. The more we develop these capabilities, the more momentum they create for us in the pursuit of capturing our most capable self.

Therefore, the true difference falls between your *potential* capabilities and your *realized* capabilities. Inside each of us exist a deep potential waiting to be discovered and unleashed. But how are you fueling it? Is it connected to your most abundant power source to propel this journey?

At times, almost everyone is capable of being incredibly confident, adaptable, resilient, focused, and motivated. Under the right circumstances, one may even behave like a world-class leader.

However, very few people execute these capabilities at full capacity. Most of the time, we can't even reach the 50% threshold. On the other hand, peak performers demonstrate their capabilities at full capacity 80% to 99% of the time, which distinguishes them from average performers. The same phenomenon exists in business, sports, performing arts, and every other area of life that requires consistent application of knowledge and abilities through language and actions. As a result, most people see a gap existing between their *potential* capabilities and their *realized* capabilities. A transcendence gap that we as individuals must seek to understand.

Capability: an intrinsic characteristic which expands your ability to perform a specific skill or set of skills.

This book will present you the knowledge and application needed to expand, improve, and maximize your capabilities. Of course, how you fuel your capabilities has the greatest impact on your end result.

DEFINITIONS

Capability Fuel

The energy source that maximizes and refines your capabilities.

Capability

An intrinsic characteristic that expands your ability to perform a specific skill or set of skills.

Imagine a high-performance sports car like a Ferrari. When properly fueled, a Ferrari can accelerate from zero to sixty mph within three seconds, whereas fueling the car with sugar water will destroy the engine before you reach the end of the block. Similarly, you can only go so far with your existing approach to your capabilities. Eventually, how you fuel these capabilities is what makes the difference.

For the most part of my entrepreneurial career, I've had a lot of my focus on human potential. After years of study, I'm convinced that the difference in capability fueling is why many otherwise smart and hard-working people struggle to maintain above average results, while peak performers enjoy dream-like success. If you picked up this book, I bet you desire for your best days to happen more often. Believe me, you already have the capabilities to make that a reality and only two things stand in your way: Awareness and Choices.

Fuel Your Choices

As I studied high performers, I found a combination of new knowledge to fuel high performance habits, plenty of marketing junk, and some false beliefs that were deeply ingrained into my subconscious. Among these learnings, some common threads of information proved true to develop and transform someone's capabilities, to elevate their ability, and to create the life they desired.

The best guidelines for abundant transformation already lie in ancient wisdoms and modern sciences. My mission was to discover and share that knowledge with you.

The principle is simple. A gap exists between our current capabilities and our true potential. Regardless of the goal, we must transcend through this difference, increase our performance, and maximize the probability of optimal outcomes by tapping into certain capabilities known to propel performance.

The process begins with developing a thorough understanding of our current abilities. At the same time, you educate yourself with the distance between your realized and your ideal self. Next, begin to build momentum with consistency. Perseverance and self-discipline are the indestructible bridge-pairing that will bring you to the other side of the gap.

Our time on this planet is limited. Therefore, it is of the upmost importance that you act upon your life goals, make the right choices, and create an environment that fosters your growth.

Ask yourself. When was the last time you consciously assessed how you responded to different stimuli you encountered? When was the last time you broke down your impulses with reason? Remember, the choices are yours and each choice you make creates a pathway. Some lead to self-destruction, materialism, fatigue, illness, and a lack of positive energy. Others lead to abundance, awareness, excellence, and mindfulness.

Since our choices dictate our life, it's vital that we do all we can to increase our ability to handle impulses and make appropriate, conscious choices.

Our mental, physical, spiritual status, and social well-being play a significant role in the choices we make every day. Books and successful individuals iterate daily how we must decide where we want to go before changing our situation, which is true. However, the key ingredient that allows you to understand and envision your desired direction, while providing the faith that makes dreams come true, is left out in these conversations.

To make any change happen, ***you*** must be the initiation. You must begin with fueling your most physiologically and spiritually abundant self, while stimulating your most driven characteristics. From that point on, you must work on it daily. Only when you transform your thinking will your thoughts become more transcendent as well. Sometimes, the progress is different from the actual shift in mindfulness. Rather, minor discipline adjustments are what move us forward most optimally. Overtime, the momentum builds up and small adjustments turn into massive transcendence. Only then are you fueling the capabilities that will catapult you and those around you, most effectively.

The more I study, the more I can support the leaders and entrepreneurs I work with, with this knowledge. Including myself, who has battled to maintain the most optimal habits for mind, body, spirit and social abundance consistently.

While business knowledge can help one professionally, personal development keeps one's performance at its highest level. Neglecting certain areas of your overall well-being will eventually creep up on you and the way you fuel each tank determines what capabilities are discovered and unleashed.

As I continued to coach others and develop my signature training program, I began to implement the ideas in this book. I found out more about what worked, what failed, what needed adjustment, and what needed supplemented.

My study of the human mind furthered and I gradually learned how we can intentionally redesign our deepest subconscious impulses to make ourselves more disciplined and consciously productive. Like Napoleon Hill said in his book *Think and Grow Rich*: "Whatever the mind of man can conceive and believe, it can achieve."

Certainly, this quote has some limitations. For example, not everyone has the genetics to make it to the NBA and the world certainly has its barriers in place resisting our push for more at certain locations. But for the most part, if you want to achieve a specific goal or intention and you believe you have the capacity to obtain it, it usually comes down to "what price you are willing to pay" to achieve this desired goal. Some goals could be as simple as improving memory or your ability to learn at an optimal level. We may each have a different capacity level to achieve a specific outcome, but there are keys to unlocking your capacity potential and raising the bar. In addition, you can develop certain capabilities with the help of the proper fuels to achieve these goals. Think of this fuel as your ***challenge fuel***. But also your ***launch fuel***.

It's your ***Level Up fuel***

Fuel you need to battle uncertainty, doubt and the challenges that present themselves each day, especially as you pursue unknown journeys, outside your comfort zone.

Professional athletes need specific fuels to manage a long and healthy career. They need to perform at optimal levels while minimizing recovery time and injury. In other professions, individuals are most focused on public speaking, communication, community uplifting, creative and critical thinking, empathetic leadership, and much more. Many individuals are chasing high performance in at least one area of their life and many of the same fuels are used intentionally to create a desired result.

Let's be honest, some of us make life harder than it needs to be. I for one have certainly been guilty of this several times. The more friction your body, mind, spiritual, social, and financial self are challenged with, the more you'll need a fuel combination to propel you forward most optimally. Whatever your path is, there are fuels that will help you through these challenges and keep you fighting the good fight.

So... what do you want to achieve?

Are you trying to maximize your ability to learn new things efficiently and effectively?

Do you seek stress management capabilities? More balance in life? A promotion or an income goal?

Do you seek better memory, improved mental performance, or additional mental toughness?

Do you want to defy aging, minimize body fat, reduce inflammation, or generate more energy in a natural way?

Do you seek to build a stronger immune system with a more resilient body?

Do you want to become more empathetic, creative, or spiritually awakened?

Are you looking to maximize your leadership ability?

Do you want closer relationships and greater trust among your family, friends, and professional network?

Regardless of your goal, this deep dive into ancient wisdom and modern science is designed to make your journey more fulfilling and successful.

Writing this book has been one beautiful, out of my comfort zone, journey. My hope is for this book to find you somewhere on your journey, while helping you fuel the outcomes you desire. Most likely, you already have many valuable skills in your personal and professional toolbox. The bigger question is whether you have the necessary capabilities to make the most of these skills.

This is what *Capability Fuel* is all about. It taps into and maximizes the energy that will enhance and refine your intrinsic capabilities. So…

…are you fueling a **Furnace** or a **Generator**?

Recall your best day again.

Imagine what would happen if a team of health experts, psychologists, neurologists, and spiritual mentors had carefully analyzed your behaviors leading up to that day. Would they identify a pattern in how you fueled your brain, body, spirit, and social network up until then? The answer is yes. Great performances are the cumulative result of trivial daily actions. Thus, you need to become aware of said actions so you can intentionally cultivate them into beneficial habits. Over time, you must adjust the fuels used and their quantities. From this day on, fuel management will forever be part of your most abundant journey.

From my observation, most people don't fuel their "Capability Tanks (brain, body, spirit, and social network)" with the intention to experience their peak days more frequently. Most of us treat these Capability Tanks like furnaces. We grab whatever crude fuel we have access to and throw it into the tanks, hoping to solve the most urgent problem of the moment. Well, furnaces burn up whatever they get. When they're done, they either burn out or demand more things to burn, until one day we realize that we've wasted years or decades burning fuels to barely stay warm, not to mention that the more you age, the harder it becomes to keep your personal furnaces burning optimally.

In the meantime, have you ever met someone who appears to be an infinite source of positivity and momentum? That's because they are properly fueling their Capability Tanks.

Fortunately, this book will teach you how to treat your Capability Tanks like generators and "smart devices" that, with appropriate fuels supported with effective processes, will reach their most abundant capacities. In return, you will consistently generate the positive energy and momentum needed to create above-average results and maximized performances. By the time you complete reading this book, you'll be more efficient with fueling so you have more "best days" regularly. You'll become a generator of positive energy for yourself and everyone around you, and generators, when properly fueled and maintained, are a powerful and independent source of sustainable energy.

Our bodies are smart devices that can be easily manipulated from external or internal forces, or mastered and managed for optimal performance. Our greatest challenge working against us is our inability to understand thyself in this time. Sure, we are all smart beings, but we also are still at the early stages of understanding the full extent of how we operate and why people do what they do. Peak performers seek to maximize that understanding, while disciplining themselves to achieve ideal outcomes. There comes a time in everyone's life that they start to decline in certain areas of their life. This is usually where the journey begins for a lot of these peak performers. The awareness sets in and they're set into a mission to flip the decline back into inclined performance.

Thus, think about what it would be like if you could have more of your best days more frequently. For a third time, go back to that best day. What were you doing? Who were you with? How did you feel? Why were you feeling that way? How was your physical and mental health? Now, think about your mission statement. Imagine living it. Let that become your fuel for applying the information in this book.

Your most abundant life is closer than you think. Are you ready to find out?

What's Your Primary Intention?

Imagine spending a few years cultivating habits that will turn you into your ***super*** self. Imagine if you get to live in your most abundant, supercharged body, mind, and social circle, even if it's only for one day. Now imagine returning to your current situation that next day. Would the glance into your most abundant life motivate you to take action? I bet it would. I bet you would feel determined to make your potential life come true. The taste and window into that life would elevate your motivation to make this a reality. Remember how that motivation feels. That's the kind of motivation you will have by the time you finish this book.

As we get started, find a specific goal for yourself. We'll call this goal your "***Primary Intention***." If you already have a Primary Intention, take the time to write it down on a piece of paper and put it somewhere you can see each morning. This will keep your mind focused until your brain is obsessed enough to constantly apply the strategies you learn in this book. If your Primary Intention isn't strong enough, your motivation to push yourself out of your comfort zone and level up your habits, will dissipate over time. Your need to accomplish this Primary Intention will have to be persuasive enough, day to day, to continue to pursue this novel mission that you set out for. Instilling new habits can be extremely difficult so you'll need to find a near obsession and necessity with your intention, to manifest its ultimate outcome.

What's Your Ultimate Win?

How would you simplify the journey you are on? How can we simplify how you will use this knowledge to "frame-in" the mission you are setting out to achieve?

As you navigate through this book, work to gain clarity on what you will be tying the knowledge you gain in this book to. What are you trying to accomplish? What's your ultimate win? Is it the person you become on the journey or is it the destination that matters more to you?

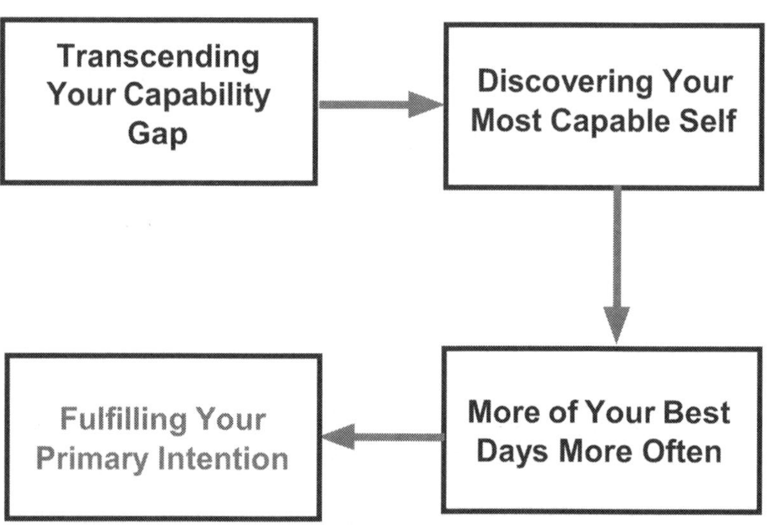

CHAPTER 2

YOUR FIVE PRIME CAPABILITIES

"If I have the belief that I can do it, I shall surely acquire the capacity to do it even if I may not have it at the beginning."

- Mahatma Gandhi

Prime Capability

Drives your effectiveness in everything you do and expands your ability to perform a specific skill orset of skills to unlock your deep potential, especially when under high pressure.

This book arms you with profound knowledge and practical strategies to optimize your "Five Prime Capabilities." A Prime Capability drives your effectiveness in everything you do and expands your ability to perform a specific skill or set of skills to unlock your deep potential, especially when under high pressure. When all five of your Prime Capabilities are working together, they create an entourage effect in your performance by activating your "Master Capability." This is how your Prime Capabilities will catapult you to a new level of personal and professional success. These are your LEVEL UP capabilities. These Five Prime Capabilities have been researched and discussed through ancient text and still hold true today through modern science as five of the most essential capabilities for human development, continued performance and momentum creation. All five of these capabilities have fuel components directly tied to the Fuel Tanks we'll discuss throughout this book.

Understanding the complexities of these capabilities and learning how to fuel them most effectively, provides a playbook for capturing your most capable self and achieving intentional goals.

Let me introduce the Five Prime Capabilities and why they're essential to your personal and professional performance.

Prime Capability #1: Confidence

Confidence

A feeling of self-assurance rising from appreciation of your abilities or qualities. Trust and belief in yourself and in your ability to meet life's challenges, and to succeed.

Confidence is the skeleton key that unlocks all your skills, knowledge, and experience, which all bolster your confidence in return. When these aspects are supported by a deep sense of self-worth, everything you do becomes easier, more effective, and more enjoyable.

Confidence gets you out of your comfort zone and into the unknown, to pursue your ideal goals and life experiences. When you're confident about pursuing new and challenging ventures, you increase your ability to have new experiences and achieve desired goals, no matter how daunting the path may seem. Consequently, your life is way more likely to change for the better.

You must have heard the saying "if you do what you've always done, you'll get what you've always gotten." It is true.

It is also true that, if you have the confidence to pursue challenging and new ventures, you will have the opportunity to achieve things you never did. Think about what this means in relation to the Primary Intention we discussed in the previous chapter. Whether your intention is an income goal, a relationship goal, or a personal health goal, my guess is that it's something you haven't experienced. Or you've had a taste of it and want the full experience. With this, you will need to do things you've probably never done to accomplish this goal. Thus, confidence becomes a vital capability for achieving your most abundant life.

Many people didn't end up with their Primary Intentions. Instead, having the confidence to try new things attracted something far better into their life — something so amazing that they never imagined it. You'll find a perfect example from the book *Three Cups of Tea*. It tells the true story of humanitarian missionary Greg Mortenson. His goal was to conquer the K2 Mountain Summit, located on the China-Pakistan border. He had never done anything similar. While he had the confidence to give it a shot, he failed to reach the top. Nonetheless, during his journey, he stumbled upon a tiny village in one of the most destitute areas of Pakistan's Karakoram Himalaya region. The villagers helped him to regain his physical strength and recover from his failed mission. Before his departure, Greg Mortenson promised to change his and the villager's lives by building a school in the area. The book continued to tell the story of how this promise became his life mission. Mortenson confronted his lifetime mission face-to-face even after he failed his original goal. In the end, he went on to become one of the most recognized humanitarians of the 20th Century. This is an example of how the confidence to try something daring and new led someone into totally unknown territories.

The "unknown" has been depleting human confidence from the beginning of time. "What you don't know" is usually coupled with a lack of confidence, doubt and fear. People want some level of predictability toward a successful outcome, but how do you predict something you've never tried? In addition, if you allow it, this new journey into uncharted waters could completely embarrass you if you fail. That's the importance of gaining confidence in your ability to figure things out, problem solve, and handle uncomfortable situations.

Confidence is built and comes in all shapes and sizes. Some individuals are lucky enough to develop it at an early age while others didn't have the same experience through their childhood. Even if you had it at an early age, there will be times you are tested and fail, and getting back up can be difficult at times. Regardless, it's up to you to build it and understand its complexities.

The more experience you expose yourself to, the more you gain confidence in your ability to battle and to navigate through the unknown. The more you battle unknown territories, the more you learn to adapt, while increasing your confidence to handle novel challenges. It's a process many entrepreneurs discuss as, "getting comfortable with the uncomfortable".

Of course, it is my hope and conviction for the ideas and knowledge in this book to empower you to achieve your Primary Intention or goal at hand. My point is that having the confidence to venture into unknown territory could lead you into a dream so much bigger or different than the one you started out with. Having the confidence in yourself to navigate through the beginning and uneasy times, will serve you many times over. Therefore, it's important to not allow a poor performance or any other failures to affect the confidence that you bring to your pursuits. Indeed, you may not have succeeded to the level that you wanted, but you are still on your journey for that success. Your confidence to try and keep trying IS the confidence that has propelled every success story.

Building confidence is a private journey. We as humans gain confidence from personal performance and our ability to maintain self-discipline. If you're someone who struggles with confidence, there's a high probability this comes from a self-reflection of a past performance, a lack of self-discipline or self-esteem. The absence of self-care creates a broken tank that leaks the fuel you need, that mind tactics alone can't repair. Your ability to keep growing by making mini-discipline adjustments is one of the keys to building self-confidence. This will develop your self-belief and keep the fuel working for you, instead of against you.

This journey is best served by applying effective processes and wisdom from past ventures to support your navigation on your next journey. The more experience you gain from struggling, winning, and learning what not to do, the more you develop situational awareness, knowledge and confidence for your next pursuit. The more you develop your situational awareness, the more you can develop a winning strategy for your journey. As an individual makes progress, they naturally gain confidence along the way. If you're able to make mini-discipline adjustments as you go, this will manifest trust in yourself to pursue the paths you desire, more frequently. For many, building confidence is about building confidence in their habits. If you're confident in your habits, you naturally build confidence for new and unknown situations that appear throughout your journey. Confidence manifests where self-discipline exists.

In conclusion, the first and most essential type of confidence, is the confidence in yourself to pursue novel and desired ventures. New ventures require courage, and courage requires confidence.

The second type of confidence is the confidence to perform under pressure and in novel situations. If you are experimenting new things, you inevitably face some new situations. People lacking the second type of confidence constantly feel like they're performing at a fraction of their full potential. In her book *Choke*, Dr. Sian Beilock, an expert on performance and brain science, revealed a common thread between students, salespeople, performers, athletes, and businesspeople who failed to perform at their maximum potential when under pressure.

Remember taking exams in school? Did you ever feel like you'd forgotten most of what you studied once the pressure was on? Ever left a job interview thinking you could have done better? If these sound familiar, you're not alone. Practically, every person in every profession knows what it's like to "choke" under pressure. Think of a salesman who knows his product inside out and who has hundreds of closing techniques memorized. He's sharp as a tack during sales meetings and role-playing sessions, and has a quick, confident response to all common objections. But when he stands in front of a real prospect, his lack of self-confidence makes him "choke." He seems to "forget" most of what he knows about selling and falls back on mediocre negotiation habits.

Occasionally, he performs at 80% to 90% of his potential for a few days or even a week. Every time this happens, he amazes the rest of the sales team with his daily or weekly results. But his sales numbers are only slightly better than the rest of his team over the long haul because his fleeting confidence leads to fleeting success.

Confidence is the one capability most people wish they had in more abundance — both the confidence to pursue desired goals and to perform under pressure.

Confidence is not just a mindset, but a capability that is developed over time. You can't fool yourself with positive thinking to behave like a confident person. If you must fool or trick your brain to believe you are more confident than you are, your confidence probably isn't deep enough. Confidence is built from your daily actions and how you see yourself.

This book gives you the knowledge and strategies needed to make this happen, so you can capture more opportunities and live a more abundant life. As you navigate on this path to building pure confidence, you'll have to understand the disguises that can cloud what we think is pure confidence. Ego and pride are great examples. Many of us use these in combination with confidence, but they can misguide and lead you to destructive behaviors. These destructive behaviors will surely interfere as you generate momentum. Taking pride in your work, life, and relationships is highly recommended, but don't let that pride mislead your true intentions. Don't get me wrong, ego and pride have propelled many successful individuals forward into successful careers, because these are forms of self-belief, and ultimately drive people. As much as they are forms of confidence and self-belief, they're also not the cleanest form of confidence that you can provide yourself and they come with side effects along the way if not properly managed. This is why we must try to develop pure confidence along the way, which is a personal journey of fueling your most sustainable, self-disciplined self.

You will also have to be careful of the confidence complex as it pertains to others. While people are attracted to confident people, some may see you as a threat or an energy source depleting their tank, due to their insecurities. People are envious of confident people and don't always like to see others happy. Understand that there will always be someone out there who wants to poke holes in your tank. If you let it happen, your confidence is clearly not internally grounded enough. Anyone's discomfort with your confidence is their problem, not yours.

Therefore, developing your internal confidence complex is a capability development journey, and not just a mindset. Its complexities are robust and it's the launching-pad for all your capability development. The more you learn and take ACTION by implementing a transformational mindset, the more you'll develop your confidence in yourself to navigate your ideal journey. Developing this confidence with a strong sense of self-awareness and an awareness to understand your environment around you, is the starting block to unlocking your capability potential at full force. The more you develop this confidence complex, the more it directly impacts your capabilities, especially the one most intricately connected to it, adaptability.

Prime Capability #2: Adaptability

Adaptability

Your ability and willingness to adjust to new conditions and realities.

In a world that is changing faster than it ever has, adaptability has never been more important. Adaptability is the catalyst for confidence. It determines the difference between your potential performance and consistent performance. Adaptability decides how you handle unexpected events, new challenges, abrupt changes in your plans, or personal crisis. Without adaptability, you're limited to very narrow personal and professional opportunities. In fact, sometimes a lack of adaptability can *appear* as lacking confidence.

Remember what I said about having the confidence to try new things? It also requires adaptability. The better you can adapt to these new experiences, while problem solving effectively, the more opportunities you will be rewarded.

Before any further explanations, let's look at one of the most no-nonsense examples of adaptability at work.

Navy Seals must pass an intensive 24-week Basic Underwater Demolition school[i], followed by a 28-week qualification training program. Apart from role-playing and virtual reality training, none of the training happens under combat conditions. Yet by the time they enter a real combat situation, their life and their comrades' lives all depend on their ability to adapt to the most stressful, unpredictable, and unimaginable conditions within seconds. How do they adapt to completely new situations on a moment's notice, especially when their lives are on the line? They are deliberately trained to fuel their adaptability through a series of specific habits and problem solving techniques.

Adaptability is also crucial in the business world. It determines how companies respond to long- and-short-term economy fluctuations, and the inevitable changes in their industry. In this new era of artificial intelligence, robots, space exploration, online shopping and a globalist view to sustainability here on earth, being adaptable has never been more important. As an individual but also as an organization. Companies that can't adapt will eventually become irrelevant and even go bankrupt. For example, a 2016 article in *Forbes* magazine[ii] shows that, of all the companies listed in the

Fortune 500 in 1955, only 61 (or 12%) remained on that list until 2014. The other 88% either merged with other companies, went bankrupt, or suffered massive revenue losses. Less than one percent of companies ever make the Fortune 500 list, meaning these are the best of the best in American business. Yet nearly 90% of them eventually fell from grace due to their long-term failure to adapt to new business environments and to stay relevant.

This is even more important today than it was over the past 50 years. Modern businesses use the “Agile” or “Waterfall” methodologies to continuously adapt to new and evolving technologies. These methodologies provide a way to develop software for continually evolving end users and to maximize end user experience. Without this approach, a company could be at risk of losing market share to the many software companies using global data to advance product offerings. Often, adaptation also means modifying the company culture and work procedures. Modern companies who practice this are even more effective than the highly adaptable companies throughout the previous century. The same goes with your personal and professional life. Changes happen. Unexpected things happen. Your ability to implement flexible and adaptable problem solving skills in both arenas, will tell a story about your ability to evolve to new and diverse environments. Whether you’re leading a business, a business team or yourself within a given role.

You’ve probably heard that success is about being in the right place at the right time, but this is only half of the truth. The other and more important half of that equation is your ability to leverage fleeting opportunities that lead to major breakthroughs and eventually, everlasting successes.

Dr. Phil is a good example this. Few people know that Oprah Winfrey originally hired Phillip Calvin McGraw in 1996 to assist her as an expert witness when she was sued by the beef industry. For many people, the opportunity would have ended there and all they'd have is a story about how they once bumped shoulders with Oprah. But, whether you like Dr. Phil or not, one thing you can't deny is how quickly he adapted to his new profession and image and became a frequent guest on Oprah's show. And he wasn't done there. He continued to leverage his popularity and became a best-selling author and a self-help celebrity.

Many people believe that success is all about being in the right place at the right time. Dr. Phil was indeed in the right place at the right time when Oprah hired him in 1996. But don't underestimate how hard it is to go from a professional counselor to a T.V. personality and from a T.V. personality to an author, and then a national self-help expert. Most people were granted similar "breaks" but never turned them into anything. That's the difference between being in the right place at the right time and being able to develop a single opportunity into a lifetime of success.

The biggest "breaks" that come into your life will most likely require you to adapt to a new opportunity on a moment's notice. Think about the confidence to try new things and how important that is for creating new opportunities and experiences. As you develop more experiences with your confidence, you become more resourceful. As your resourcefulness develops, it directly fuels your adaptability. When confidence and adaptability are working together, you can open doors in your life that are currently blocked off by obstacles. If you fail to rise to the occasion, the opportunity will pass, leaving you kicking yourself for not being "ready." You've probably already missed at least one big opportunity like this. We all have. However, by reading and using the strategies in this book, you'll be prepared to seize and leverage these encounters to create bigger opportunities, and to domino them into lasting success. That's the tangible power of adaptability.

Prime Capability #3: Resilience

Resilience

Your ability to recover and overcome difficulties and challenges.

Resilience is the ability to maintain your core values and stick to your commitments in the face of failure, adversity, and success. You may be surprised that I included success in this list but it takes resilience to handle success without becoming egotistical and ruining yourself in the process. If you need an example, watch a few episodes of the show "Behind the Music." You'll find story after story where superstar musicians rise to fame, only to crash and burn because of their inability to responsibly manage that success. Resilience determines how quickly you recover after getting knocked down, and whether you get back up as a better or worse version of yourself. More importantly, it also gives you the emotional fortitude to effectively manage success.

When legendary boxer Mike Tyson[iii] hit the scene in his early 20's, he was practically invincible. He knocked out some opponents so fast, fight attendees would demand refunds because it was over so quickly. Unfortunately, Mike never quite recovered his original mojo after losing to Buster Douglas. After serving a couple years in prison, he damaged his boxing career further by going Hannibal Lector on Evander Holyfield as he took a bite out of his ear. Decades later, in an interview with Dan LeBatard from "The Art of Conversation," Mike said that his ego had given him everything he wanted when he was young, but his coach never gave him the tools to "shut off" his ego. That turned out to be a problem for Mike's sterling athletic career. As he said himself in the 2019 interview:

"I was groomed to be Goliath. I wasn't groomed to be David. I was groomed to be Goliath because I was so insecure. I was a monster. That's all I really know and that's all I wanted to be because that's what the most successful fighters were. I was a Goliath, a killer and no one was gonna feel sorry for me."

Since the revelation, Mike Tyson became more spiritually aware. He's still one hell of a fighter, even at age fifty. His early life is an example of how ego can get you to a certain level of success, but resilience is what keeps you there. It proves that ego is the enemy of resilience. Confidence, on the other hand, combined with adaptability, produces the resilience to turn failure and success into lasting achievements and deep personal fulfillment. While I was putting the finishing touches on this book, Mike Tyson announced he'd be climbing back into the ring to fight the all-time great boxer Roy Jones Jr. This took an amazing amount of resilience and determination for a 54-year-old athlete. But this is what happens when someone finally conquers false, ego-driven confidence, and discovers a deeper source of personal power. It's an example of confidence and resilience working together.

Nonetheless, resilience doesn't always mean making a big comeback. More often, it's the power to stay on course for the long haul. Another star boxer, George Foreman[iv], enjoyed a long and successful career spanning from his first fight in 1969 to his final match in 1997 when he was nearly 50 years old. This was three years after he won the heavyweight championship by defeating Michael Moorer. Moorer had a 35-0 record going into the fight, but Foreman had spent his career building up to that victory. That takes more than just physical resilience.

Mike Tyson and George Foreman were both incredibly talented, tough, and hard-working. They each applied resilience in different ways. One of them had the resilience to stay in the sport for decades and became the oldest heavyweight champion in history. The other demonstrated resilience by battling, and finally overcoming his ego to discover a deeper and more sustainable source of personal power.

Another story of resilience takes us on a journey of overcoming extreme difficulties with several prime capabilities. At the young age of 8, Ping Fu was ripped from her mother's arms and placed onto a train of strangers during China's Cultural Revolution. Her next stop was unknown. Greeted by a group of teenagers in uniforms, she was dropped off at a dormitory filled with lost children. In this dormitory she shared a small and dirty room with a couple other kids, and it became their home for the next decade. The bare concrete floors and wretched sleeping conditions were just part of the struggle as she and her companion's battled starvation and child abuse. During the day, she was summoned to a child labor factory and she eventually became a soldier. Somehow through her rigor and abysmal situation, she never lost hope and the desire to pursue her education, and her goals to make it to America. At the age of 25 with $80 to her name, she made it to America and worked her way through school as a computer programmer, while learning to speak English.

She went on to become the founder and CEO of Geomagic, a leading software company in 3D printing and imaging. She was named Entrepreneur of the Year in 2005 by *Inc* magazine and sat on the Innovation and Entrepreneurship Council for President Obama during his term.

In 2013, her company Geomagic was acquired by 3D Systems Inc, where she took the reins as Vice President and Chief Entrepreneur Officer. You can take a deeper dive into her story of resilience and adaptability to change in her memoir *Bend, Not Break*, published in 2013. She walked a remarkable journey from despair to triumph. To be able to sustain so much trauma and abuse only to go on to accomplish what she has, took proper fuels to keep moving forward. People that know her describe her as possessing extreme generosity, distinguished intelligence, and unmatched resilience. Her ability to remain hopeful and loving, helped her escape her insufferable reality and allowed her to make it to America to pursue the American Dream.

With the right combination of confidence, adaptability, and resilience, you will turn into a champion in whatever you choose to do next, especially when you combine them with the next two capabilities, to activate your Master Capability. Resilience empowers you to turn your failures, battles, and successes into steppingstones toward bigger accomplishments. Failure can change you. So can success. The question is whether you become better with each new challenge, opportunity, and success, or if you lose your momentum and never get it back. Again, this book gives you the practical habits so you can stay resilient in the face of all of these. If you develop your capability to be resilient and persist on your journey, each new hardship and success will lead you closer to your most abundant life.

The journey is different for each of us and requires a slightly different makeup for optimal performance, but resilience is needed for everyone's journey. Imagine what will happen in your life once you start fueling your most durable resilient capabilities.

Prime Capability #4: Focus

Focus

The state of producing clear visuals. The ability to concentrate your attention and energy on a singlegoal for a prolonged period.

Focus is another capability almost everyone wished they had in more abundance, for good reason. It magnifies your results by concentrating all your energy and capabilities on your true ambitions. If you spend a few hours in direct sunlight, you might get a mild sunburn. Take that same light and focus it onto one spot, and you've got yourself a laser capable of cutting through a steel door. Likewise, when people focus all (or most) of their attention and energy on a single goal until they win, they can overcome almost any obstacle. On the other hand, people who lack focus may have short bursts and waves of success, followed by extended periods of mediocrity and depression. You can find successful people with low confidence or lacking basic people skills. You can even find successful people with only an average talent in their field. But I challenge you to find a consistently successful person who lacks the capability to focus.

In *Think and Grow Rich*, Napoleon Hill tells the amazing story of Edwin C. Barnes and his lifetime aspiration to become Thomas Edison's business partner. When Barnes went to work for Edison, he started out as a mere salesperson. His opportunity finally came when Edison was preparing to launch a new office device, the Dictating Machine (later, it became known as the "Ediphone.") Edison's salespeople weren't interested in selling the invention because they believed it would take a miracle for it to sell. But Barnes saw this as an opportunity to get Edison's attention with his ability to succeed when everyone else was making excuses. Barnes approached Edison with a marketing plan for the device, got it approved, and sold it so well that Edison gave him an exclusive contract to sell the device. The device became so popular that it inspired a new slogan in the marketplace "Made by Edison, Installed by Barnes."

This story teaches many lessons, the most important one being that Barnes was prepared for this rare and unexpected opportunity because he never took his focus off his goal of going into business with Edison. If he'd lost that focus, he might have viewed the Ediphone as a dead duck product that wouldn't earn them any commission like Edison's other salespeople. Barnes responded to this opportunity and turned it into a long-term success because he focused on his goal until the right door opened. This is a brilliant example of confidence, adaptability, and focus working together.

Now, think about all the time, energy, and money you've wasted switching between tasks, changing your goals, or even changing your mind about your career path or your life purpose. Compare this to Edwin C. Barnes' story and ask yourself how many opportunities have slipped right past you without you recognizing them until it was too late simply because you weren't focused at the time. Your mind has an uncanny ability to draw your attention to the things it focuses on the most. It also has a stunning ability to bring opportunities consistent with the things you focus on achieving into your life.

Most individuals that achieve monumental success on a given path, have taken their focus to an obsession level. Their ability to get obsessed with their work is their superpower. Not all journeys are created equal though. There's a large difference between someone getting obsessed with professional basketball and someone in a job they extremely dislike. At least for me, the opportunity to play basketball or to build my own company, would be far easier to get obsessed with than becoming obsessed with a job that didn't interest me. But if this job reality is your situation, that's the intention of this book, giving you the motivation and manual for how to seek out that mission that inspires you, while providing the fuels necessary to handle the challenging road you'll discover on your path. Find a level of desperation or obsession with figuring out a path you desire and the focus will follow. The mental state of being desperate will trigger alert chemicals to help you move forward, no matter what presents itself.

The more clarity and focus you bring to your intentions, the more they will serve and fuel the rest of your Prime Capabilities as you navigate your journey. As you do this, you will inspire others to do the same and will naturally develop your final Prime Capability, leadership.

Prime Capability #5: Leadership

Leadership

Your ability to lead, motivate, and inspire desiredoutcomes. The ability to recognize and develop talent.

There's only one thing more powerful than performing like a champion when it really counts, adapting to new environments effectively, and staying focused on the mission at hand. That one thing is the ability to use the other four capabilities to organize, inspire, and motivate others to do the same for themselves. If you can lead a group of people to perform at 80% to 90% of their potential while working towards a common goal, while manifesting abundance in trust and teamwork, there's practically no limit to what you can achieve.

Think about Mahatma Gandhi, the Indian lawyer and political ethicist who used nonviolent resistance to lead India out of British oppression. He led millions of people to work together courageously and persistently to achieve a common goal. Nearly a century later, people are still studying and applying his ideas and strategies to political movements everywhere. What's shocking is that Mahatma Gandhi was not your stereotypical leader portrayed in Hollywood movies or best-selling novels. He was so shy and timid around people that he would run from school back home, fearing someone might try to talk to him. In his autobiography, *The Story of My Experiments With Truth*, Gandhi shares how quiet and reserved he was around people that he sometimes has to write down his thoughts and read them off a paper if he had to make a particularly important point.

Despite his lack of traditional charisma, Gandhi's commitment to personal discipline turned him into one of the most influential people in history. His "Experiments with Truth" often involved personal experiments, like training his taste buds to become accustomed to bland foods and eat them without seasonings. Gandhi's story is a good example of what Stephen R. Covey refers to as turning "personal victories" into "public victories." In other words, his commitment to master his own habits gave birth to his ability to organize, inspire, and motivate others. Likewise, your ability to fuel your Prime Capabilities of confidence, adaptability, resilience, and focus will give birth to the Prime Capability called Leadership.

Leadership is both a personal and social journey. Before you can have true social leadership, your ability to lead yourself, must be developed and sharpened. People want to follow someone stronger than themselves. Your ability to transcend your leadership capacity gap, by consciously acting on your own self-leadership journey, plays the largest role in your ability to gain influence. Once you've developed your own self-leadership capabilities, developing the necessary social leadership capabilities will come more organically. Mastering one's own journey breeds success and light for others to follow.

In this new digital arena, with working from home becoming more prevalent, leadership has never been more important as well. Keeping your team healthy, working together effectively and maintaining a desired quality of culture has certainly been challenged with the new circumstances surrounding the pandemic and working from home. Virtual Leadership has created challenges, a feeling of disconnect and often times a lack of awareness into team member situations. Your ability to focus and adapt to the details of your team members is critical to lead most effectively.

As this book unfolds, you'll discover two things with absolute clarity:

The first is the fact that you have leadership capabilities you never knew you had the capacity for.

Next and more importantly, you'll discover that the secret to maximizing your leadership capability comes from your ability to leverage the other four Prime Capabilities. Combining these capabilities with an aware and empathetic approach, provides an opportunity to lead most masterfully.

YOUR MASTER CAPABILITY

The goal of this book is to turn your small, daily actions into habits, and to turn those collective habits into massive, positive momentum, which makes this process easier in return. Once activated, it eventually becomes your second nature. When all five of your Prime Capabilities are working together, they create an entourage effect in your performance and activate MOMENTUM, beginning your launch into a new level of personal and professional success. How you fuel your capabilities and get them working in harmony toward a desired goal, is the process of activating and maximizing momentum.

At the beginning of this book, I asked you to imagine the most productive day of your life. Now, can you remember the most productive *period* of your life? Do you remember how excited you were, how unstoppable you felt, and how much people admired your ability to accomplish what you set out for? Whatever happened to all that momentum?

If you're asking this question, you already know how serious losing your momentum is. Careers end up chugging along for decades, never really picking up the steam again or capturing the goals you once set out for. Relationships may never recover. Dreams and opportunities that once excited, motivated, and inspired you, end up an element of your memory that can erode fulfillment potential.

At the same time, relationships, careers, dreams, and opportunities that can maintain and increase their momentum are unstoppable. They become a perpetual generator of positive energy in our lives, radiating positive influence into every other area, and receiving it back again through this entourage effect. Bottom line: momentum is your Master Capability, the magic ingredient that you can't succeed without.

While momentum is hard to build, it's even harder to reconstruct once lost. Countless extremely talented athletes, performing artists, and businesspeople have had tremendously successful "streaks," only to fall from grace and never fully recover their momentum. But if you apply this book's strategies, you'll not only activate your momentum, but also learn the habits and gain the tools that sustain and multiply it. As you do so, your momentum will continue to fuel your Five Prime Capabilities as an added fuel source. You will move beyond mental and physical limitations that held you back for years, and leap into a life of lasting success and fulfilment. Only by then will you realize that momentum is both the Master Capability and a fuel for your Five Prime Capabilities.

Is there really a formula for activating and generating momentum?

You bet there is. BUT it's usually an uncomfortable path to create momentum toward newly established goals and outcomes. Mini-discipline adjustments and transformations are usually required and most people don't enjoy change. We do things the way we already do them for a reason. Making small changes daily can be an exhausting path and turning the mini-adjustments into daily habits can come with a cost, like less time watching Netflix or hanging out at your favorite bar.

Momentum has a formula and the formula is unlocked as you gain awareness into your ability to develop your prime capabilities and to fuel these capabilities most effectively.

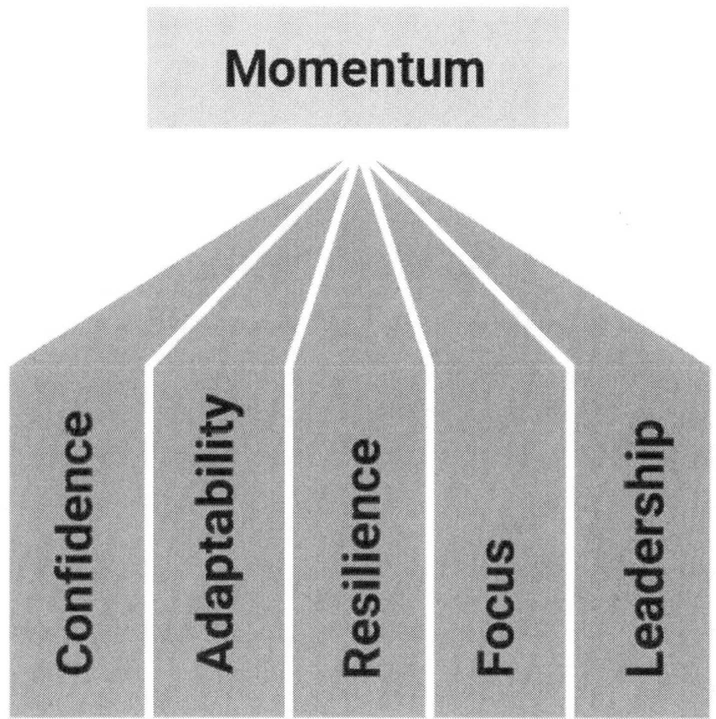

CHAPTER 3

YOUR FOUR CAPABILITY FUEL TANKS

Imagine if you could get your Five Prime Capabilities working at 80% or more of their potential for 80% or more of the time. Again, this is not an impractical promise. You've already had a few great days in your life. However, if you're like most hard-working and ambitious people, my guess is you're not nearly as consistent at getting and staying "In The Zone."

So, what's the solution?

Accessing and consciously managing your Four Capability Fuel Tanks.

Capability Fuel Tank #1: Your Brain[v]

If procrastination, self-doubt, indecisiveness, or impulsiveness are holding you back, your brain is not focusing on creating a better future for yourself.

Your brain makes up about 1% of your body weight, but it burns 20% to 25% of your daily calories. What is all that energy creating? Look at your present results and you'll have the answer. When it comes to being consistently confident, adaptive, resilient, focused, and being a highly capable leader, your brain can be your greatest asset or your worst enemy. It all depends on whether you fuel your brain for success or for self-sabotage.

Most people are not aware that our brain is doing a lot of things without our conscious "permission." For example, our nervous system sends about 11 million bits of data per second to our brain whereas our conscious mind can only process about 50 bits per second. The rest of those thought impulses (nearly 11 million bits of data) are processed subconsciously. Think of your subconscious thoughts as the "background programs" running on your computer while you're only using one application. If you're not fueling your entire brain properly, you're taking a gamble as to whether these subconscious programs are working for you or against you.

No wonder so many people never reach their most abundant potential. Most of them do not know how to fuel their brains to make the Five Prime Capabilities work in their favor for building a new future and instead return to the patterns where your brain focuses on comfortable and old "programs".

Capability Fuel Tank #2: Your Body

Your body is your brain's instrument.

The question is whether your body's functions are in harmony with your desired life. For example, everything you do starts with an action potential firing in one of your nerve cells (neurons). They send chemical or electrical messages to other neurons through synapses, which in turn send signals down their axons. These messages aren't just relayed to other neurons, but also to your muscles, vital organs, and all the important hormone secreting glands that control your endocrine system.

Therefore, view your body as a computer's network running multiple complex software programs and processing billions of pieces of data every second. As we've established, most of this is happening faster and in a greater abundance than your conscious mind could possibly control or process. Then, no wonder you can't maximize your skills and abilities by willpower and positive thinking alone.

Furthermore, an average human's digestive system contains tens of trillions of microorganisms, including an estimated 1,000 species of known bacteria and countless unknown ones. Most people don't know that our brain and gut are connected by an "information superhighway" called the Vagus nerve. This master nerve sends a variety of signals from your gut to your brain and vice versa in the same way traffic moves from one part of the town to another. Combine all the intersectional microorganic activities with the millions of neurons and trillions of cells you have, and you've got a symphony of complex data processing within you, even in your sleep. All this data processing happens too fast and too abundantly for your conscious mind to comprehend or control. Now, imagine what's happening right now with the ever-expanding Internet of Things (IoT). Millions of "smart devices" around the world tap into a global data source, each performing its individual functions while being a part of one highly "intelligent," interconnected system. As mind-boggling as this may sound, something much more complex is going on in your body right now.

Just imagine the dramatic impact this has on your ability to access the mental states that propel human progress. But how many personal development authors have told you that you can change your life by changing your ways of thinking alone? How many of them only give philosophical arguments or time-management programs for you to stick with using only your willpower? No wonder the gap between your potential capabilities and your realized capabilities is so vast. Luckily, you'll have a practical set of tools to leverage yourself to properly fuel your brain AND your body for success by the end of this book.

To think further into your body as an instrument, let's look at the attention that Lebron James and Russell Wilson have put on their body and brain. In 2019, Lebron revealed that he spends approximately $1.5 million to take care of his body, to recover, and to fuel his ultimate performance physically and mentally day after day. At the age of 35, Lebron James is still known by many as the best basketball player in the world, as he continues to fuel his body for peak performance. In 2020, he led his team, the Los Angeles Lakers to an NBA championship and people are taking notice of his "body fuel attention". Russell Wilson jumped onboard this high-performance body train and has admitted to spending $1 million on himself coming into the 2020 season. At the time of writing this book, he is the clear favorite for the MVP award this year with the Seattle Seahawks. There's clearly something to this attention on body fuels. I realize not everyone is trying to become a world-class athlete, but there's plenty to learn from how these two fuel their most resilient, durable, brain-fueling bodies. I also realize that we all don't have $1 million to spend on our body each year for optimal performance. Don't worry, this isn't necessary unless you have similar goals to them. Instead, you can utilize ancient wisdom and modern science that are far more economical for the rest of us. The largest factor is adopting these new habits that can fuel your brain and body's capability development, to capture a more abundant you.

Capability Fuel Tank #3: Your Spirit

If your body is your brain's instrument, then your brain is your spirit's instrument. People with well-fueled spirits have an astonishing ability to perform in harmony with their deepest values even when everything and everyone around them is pressuring for compromises. This ability has less to do with courage but more with one's keen awareness that there are things more important than their fear and even personal survival. These individuals also have a nearly supernatural level of confidence because they understand that there are other things larger than their fears and insecurities.

Essentially, people with properly-fueled spirits have an incredible ability to empathize with others, which is even more important than courage and confidence. Empathy provides you with the social context for applying your capabilities in a way that makes a real difference for others. This is how you create outstanding accomplishments.

The motivational legend Zig Ziglar used to say:

"You will get *all* you want *in life, if you help enough other people* get what they want.*"*

It is not only true, but also brings forward measurable results. Think about all the ultra-successful people in the past 150 years, from Thomas Edison to Steve Jobs, and you'll find that they all created things extremely useful in helping others get what they want. Of course, some manage to do this regardless of having empathy. However, empathy gives you a rare insight into human needs, which prompts you to create and provide products and services so useful in fulfilling human needs that people all over the world will gladly pay for them. That is empathy's economic benefit that you don't read much about in business books. Furthermore, empathy is also an invaluable skill in building better friendships and better marriages, being a better parent, and becoming a great leader. People with well-fueled spirits have a rare combination of courage and empathy that makes them a unique and unstoppable force in the world.

While most personal development books only deal in vague generalities on spiritual development, we're going to talk about the emerging scientific discoveries regarding the practical advantages of having your heart, brain, nervous system, and metabolism all working in harmony. Ultimately, we are talking about achieving wholeness through your connection to a higher source of awareness and power. You'll find references to the spiritual concept of wholeness in dozens of ancient texts, including *The New Testament Gospels*, Chapter Ten of *Tao Te Ching*, Chapter Seven of the *Buddhist Dhammapada*, *Hindu Upanishads*, and the *Yoga Sutras of*

Patanjali. By collecting this knowledge, this book gives you the practical explanations and strategies needed to achieve this spiritual wholeness, reach your ideal mental state, and activate your Master Capability.

Capability Fuel Tank #4: Your Social Network

This is your most critical Capability Fuel Tank. Your social network either makes or breaks your ability to consistently fuel your brain, your body, and your spirit with positive energy. It also determines how much positive energy you invest into the lives of those around you. I think we can all agree that physically healthy people tend to hang around each other in the same way that physically unhealthy people are drawn to one another. This is also true for people who are mentally, spiritually, and emotionally healthy. When you think about the people you've known who have not lived a purposeful life, I bet they started out by doing one or both of the following things first:

They started associating with the wrong people.

They stopped associating with the right people.

In my experience, the most destructive thing for your personal ambitions is to allow others to dictate your path in life or let them interfere with your mental and emotional states. Therefore, we will cover the first three Capability Tanks before finishing off with this one.

Therefore, we'll focus first on fueling your brain, body, and spirit to reach peak performance. If you take care of the first three tanks, everything you do to fuel your social network will come back to you in mind-bending abundance.

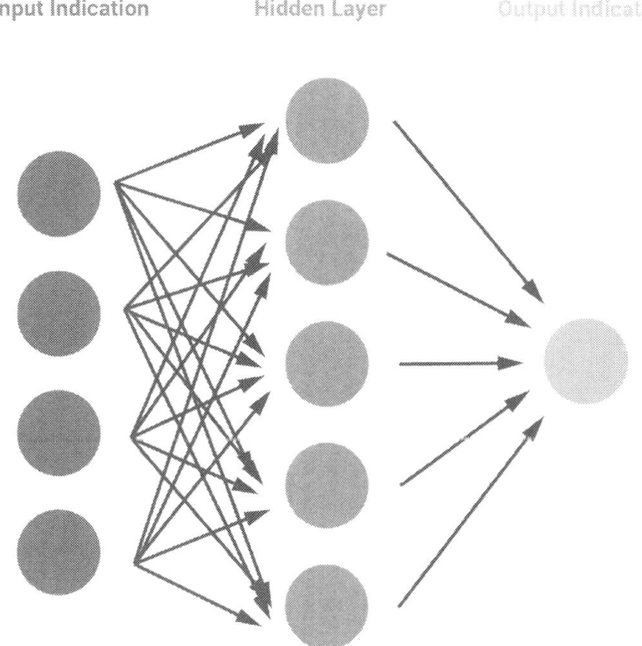

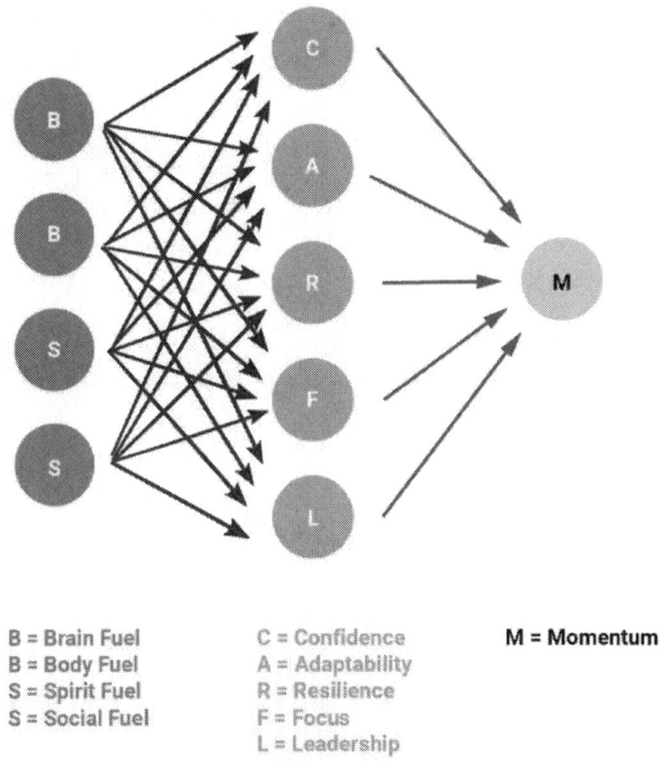

Similar to how a neural network works, so does the process of activating and generating momentum. Neural Networks form the base of deep learning, which is an artificial intelligence function of how the brain works in processing all data it's consuming. Neural Networks use a series of algorithms to understand and recognize underlying relationships in a set of data through a process that mimics how our brains work. Neural Networks take in data, train themselves to recognize the patterns in this data and predict the output from this data.

It's the same process for Momentum generation. It starts with an input. What are you welcoming into your life, your body and your brain? The habits we implement into our lives create a “fuel input”. What we download, consume and the routines we partake in on a daily basis are our inputs. The hidden layer is the processing of these inputs and where these combinations of fuels and capabilities interact to create an output. How you fuel your capabilities and get them working together synergistically, tells a story of the output (momentum) that you activate and generate. The more you input healthy and momentum creating habits, the more you’ll level up and transcend your capabilities toward Momentum.

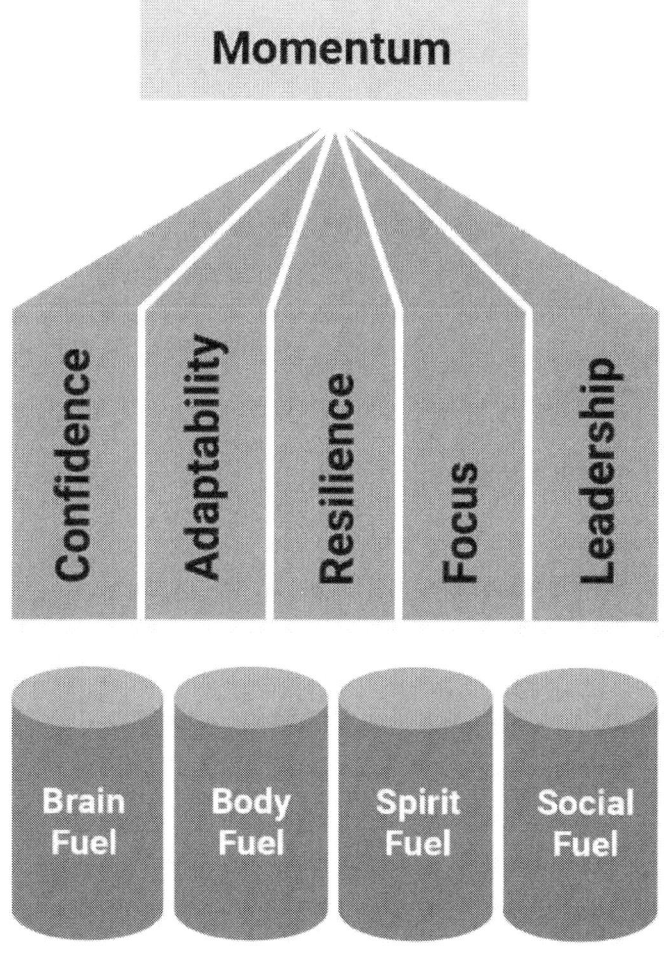

Chapter 4: Brain Fuel

"More gold has been mined from the thoughts of men than has been taken from the earth."

-Napoleon Hill

The more you perform with your mind each day, the more you must learn how to fuel it for consistent daily performances.

After thousands of years of technological innovation, your brain is still the most powerful, efficient machine in the known universe. Even artificial intelligence, as it is currently evolving, can't match the creative power of human imagination. Picture what that means if you get your brain fueled for accomplishing your life's mission. A well-fueled brain will consistently make you more confident, adaptable, resilient, focused, and a better leader.

To help you fuel your brain, we will cover:

Fueling your mental state

Building your mental framework

You might have heard the term "mental toughness." But how often do you hear about how to become mentally tough? Not so much, right?

To build a strong mentality, you need to build your mental framework, fuel your mental state, and harmonize them for maximum performance. Think of your brain as a self-driving car. Your mental state represents how well that car runs, including the condition of its fuel performance, reliability, safety, etc. Meanwhile, your mental framework represents the car's data-driven navigational system. If the self-driving car is running like a dream but its navigational software is off or isn't collecting or processing quality data, you'll get lost. On the opposite side, if the software is up-to-date and connected to a reliable data stream, but your car's engine, transmission, or brakes are broken, you will crash or at least have a difficult time reaching your destination. Therefore, it is only when your car's navigation system and physical components are working in harmony that you will enjoy a safe, successful ride to your destination.

What's Your Ideal Mental State[vi]?

Some personal development books preach that there's only one ideal mental state where you can train yourself to live all the time. The truth is your ideal mental state varies according to what you're trying to achieve. For example, depending on how well we care for our mental health and our focus within the given activity, our brain experiences different states while sleeping, waking up, and performing activities. Therefore, your control over your mental state has a ***huge*** impact on how your Five Prime Capabilities perform.

Similarly, both learning and productivity are dependent to your mental state. But don't assume that there's only one optimal state for learning and only one for productivity. It all depends on the type of task you have or the type of learning you're doing. Think about where your mental states originated. When networks of neurons fire, they produce signals forming into measurable brain wave frequencies, like how a pianist can strike multiple keys in unison and produce a harmonious sound. Certain combinations of piano keys produce major chords which sound "happy," while others produce minor chords that sound "sad." Other combinations produce dominant 7, diminished, or augmented chords, which sound unsettling and demand a resolution so a more harmonious sound can be created. Composers weave these chords together to create "progressions." Progressions then create tension, followed by a resolution to a more harmonious chord. Composers follow these rules to create music that moves us emotionally and has a profound impact on our mental state, and even our development as a person over time. It is the same when movie directors use cliff-hanging scenes to build up anticipation before the story is finally resolved and returned to joy and harmony. Movies using these techniques can take the audience into another world and often leave a lasting impact on how they feel and what they think.

Our mental states work in a similar way. Each state serves its purpose in moving us toward our goals. Therefore, we shouldn't make the mistake of thinking there's only one ideal mental state that we should expect to live in all the time. Instead, we need to focus on managing our mental states to match our present objectives.

Let's break down different mental states in terms of their

respective brain waves.[vii]

- **Delta waves** (.5 to 3 Hz)
  The slowest brain waves that occur primarily during your deepest state of dreamless sleep.
- **Theta waves** (3 to 8 Hz)
  They happen during our sleep but have also been observed in the deepest states of Zen meditation.
- **Alpha waves** (8 to 12 Hz)
  Present when daydreaming or consciously practicing mindfulness, or during meditations. Alpha waves are also seen during aerobic exercise and are typically associated with creativity and feelings of confidence.
- **Beta waves** (12 to 30 Hz)
  Typically dominate waking states of consciousness. They occur when attention is directed toward solving a problem or avoiding a threat.

Again, your ideal mental state depends on what you're trying to achieve at the time.

For example, Beta waves are most often associated with high-pressure situations, such as trying to meet a deadline or working hard on a physically or mentally taxing problem. Returning to our prior analogy, the Beta wave state would represent those tense moments in a story or in a piece of music. This state can be useful for pushing yourself to work longer hours to wrap up a project, but it's not an ideal state of mind for creative thinking ***or*** for connecting and empathizing with other people. If you spend too much time in the Beta wave state, your sympathetic nervous system that drives your "fight or flight" instincts will remain active far longer than necessary. As a result, your body will direct its energy away from essential functions such as recovery and digestion. Eventually, you'll wear yourself out physically and mentally.

Have you've ever had extended periods of extreme productivity followed by periods of lagging motivation or depression? This happens when you spend too much time in the "fight or flight" state but not enough time in the "rest and digest" state. Occasionally, your subconscious will seek opportunities to get you out of the survival state. Sometimes, it will even sabotage your current projects to reach this goal. Maybe you become absent minded and lose a client, or hurt yourself from your lack of alertness. Or maybe you simply get distracted by a YouTube video and spend the next few hours getting sucked into video after video. In common language, this is self-sabotage. Scientifically speaking, this is your subconscious trying to get you back into a more relaxed state where your parasympathetic nervous system, which drives your resting and recovery functions, can take over and restore the equilibrium.

	Frequency	Details
Delta wave	0.5-3 Hz	The slowest brain waves that occur primarily during your deepest state of dreamless sleep.
Theta wave	3-8 Hz	They happen during our sleep but have also been observed in the deepest states of Zen meditation.
Alpha wave	8-12 Hz	Present when daydreaming or consciously practicing mindfulness, or during meditations. Alpha waves are also seen during aerobic exercise and are typically associated with creativity and feelings of confidence.
Beta wave	12-30 Hz	Typically dominate waking states of consciousness. They occur when attention is directed toward solving a problem or avoiding a threat.

Ancient mystics called these polarized states the "sacred masculine" (the fight or flight state) and the "sacred feminine" (the rest and digest state), represented by the famous Yin Yang symbol[viii], where each color represents one of the sacred energy sources. The ancient sages considered the harmonizing of these two energies the achievement of ultimate union with divinity. You'll also find a metaphorical allusion to these dual energies in Ephesians 5:22-32 in the *New Testament* when the apostle Paul talks about marriage and the mystery of godliness.

Modern scientists call the equalizing of these two physiological states "homeostasis." Regardless of the terminology, this harmonizing of states is just as necessary to your mental health as the ebb and flow of the tides, and the coming and going of the seasons. People who try to fight this and remain in the hyper-productive Beta state (sacred masculine) all the time inevitably land on the rocks. Likewise, spending too much time in the rest and digest state (sacred feminine) makes the body restless and leads to lax attitudes toward work projects and other deadline-driven activities. Therefore, it's smarter to treat these two states as equally essential energies whose natural rhythm leads you into a life of balance and growth.

Take the learning process as an example. Neuroscientists have identified different "modes" of learning, explicit and implicit. Explicit learning is conscious and deliberate. If you can consciously explain the specific steps of what you've been learning to someone else, that's explicit learning. For example, if I asked you to memorize the letters of the Greek Alphabet, the books of the Bible, or the elements in the periodic table, that would be explicit learning. Implicit learning, on the other hand, involves motor skills and cannot be communicated as easily as explicit learning, like learning to type, shoot a gun, ride a bike, or paddle a canoe, that's implicit learning.

Researchers at MIT have found that explicit and implicit learning are accompanied by their own respective brain wave patterns. But that's not all. They also discovered fluctuations in brain wave patterns depending on whether the learning was successful or unsuccessful. Tasks requiring explicit learning showed an increase in alpha2-beta brain waves (10-30 hertz) after a "correct" choice, but an increase in delta-theta waves

(3-7 hertz) after an "incorrect" choice. But the alpha2-beta waves also decreased as the learning progressed.

This is an example of how your brain waves ebb and flow as you either succeed in demonstrating a new skill, or mentally reassess after failing at it. This is a completely natural process which, when applied persistently, leads to growth of new skills and capabilities. Earl K. Miller, Professor of Neuroscience at the Picower Institute for Learning and Memory and the Department of Brain and Cognitive Sciences, said the alpha-2-beta brain waves "could reflect the building of a model of the task, and then after the animal learns the task, the alpha-beta rhythms then drop off, because the model is already built." This "model building" is similar to the development of mental frameworks.

Millar also said that the fluctuations between delta-theta rhythms increasing and decreasing might reflect neural "rewiring." Once again, we see evidence of a natural "tension and release" between mental states, just as we sense the progression between periods of tension and release when listening to music. This is the natural process of the brain growing and developing. So, let's not assume that one mental state is always ideal and pressure ourselves about being in that state all the time. It's more important to be aware of your mental states and to get them work in harmony to promote capability development. The ability to manage these mental "rhythms" is what enables you to fuel your mental states for maximum confidence, resilience, adaptability, focus, and leadership.

Fueling Your Flow State

The Flow State, also known colloquially as being "In the Zone," is the mental state in which a person performing an activity is fully immersed in a feeling of energized focus, full involvement, and enjoyment in the activity's process. This state is the union between the sacred masculine and the sacred feminine. According to modern science, it's the healthy balance of your parasympathetic and sympathetic nervous system and their corresponding brain waves.

In your Flow State, your clarity is nearly impeccable, and you're practically immune to negative thinking, self-doubt, and sometimes even to pain and fear. A stunning example of this is the Yogi master Wim Hof, known as the "Iceman," who holds the world record for cold exposure. Hof is best known for his ability to sit and meditate in only shorts and shoes in the middle of a frozen landscape without shivering or showing any physical signs associated with this type of exposure. His command over his mental and physical state is so incredible that he's been commissioned to train US Navy SEALs on his techniques. There has been a tremendous amount of information that has been uncovered recently on the power of cold exposure and breathwork. Both of which can alter mental states, and when learned to use effectively, one can use these to access heightened alertness, clarity and mind-body connection.

I'm not saying you need to meditate in the middle of a snowfield. But imagine what would happen if you could gain a fraction of this kind of control over your mental states.

Learning how to access your Flow State is similar. It's a

process of developing a practice that supports the birth of your Flow State.

Here is a step by step process that will help you get to know your own mental states:

Choose one specific task to master.

- Make sure it's something you enjoy doing.
- Set aside time to focus ONLY on practicing that task.
- Have a clear outcome in mind as you practice your task.
- Eliminate external and internal distractions.
- Make sure the task is challenging, but not too hard.
- Listen to music that puts you into a good state for that task.
- Prepare your body for these practice times (more on this later).
- Keep practicing this task until you can do it in your Flow State.

Most importantly, try to make your practice timing *and* location as consistent as possible. This will provide your brain and body with "cues" to recognize the ideal state for your selected task. For example, assume you're practicing Flow State between 7am and 8am every day, and you're doing it out of a specific location in your house. For the first few weeks, you might not notice anything unusual. But after a few practice sessions, your brain will start to associate that time frame and those outside sensations (the room, the music etc.)

as associated with the selected task and its corresponding mental state. By the time you start getting good at the task, you'll notice a change in your mental state the moment you walk into your practice area at the designated time. After enough practice you'll be able to conjure up that mental state, simply by closing your eyes and imagining yourself in that space and surrounding. This is called "neuroassociation" and it can develop your mental states the same way a piece of fitness equipment at the gym, develops a certain part of your body.

People who can access their Flow State on command show a significant gain in their performance and their happiness. Initially coined by Mihaly Csikszentmihaly, a "Flow State" is an altered state of consciousness that produces heightened levels of performance, with less effort. It can only occur when we're able to get out of our heads and turn off the inner critic (a.k.a., the ego) that creates noises and distractions. The Flow State is a state of mind where there is less friction and you're flooded with happy neurotransmitters and hormones. For example, people in the Flow State show an increase in important chemicals like dopamine (the reward chemical), serotonin (the "happy" chemical), and other key neurotransmitters and hormones. The presence of these chemicals alters your perception of reality by altering your mental state. When you're in the Flow State, your focus, clarity and your ability to perform the task at hand is magnified.

I could share a lot more examples, but this should be enough to show that you can gain control over your mental states through intentional practice. For example, as I worked on this book, one of my goals was trying to access this Flow State each morning when my brain was refreshed, while also beginning with morning routines that provided a positive chemical release.

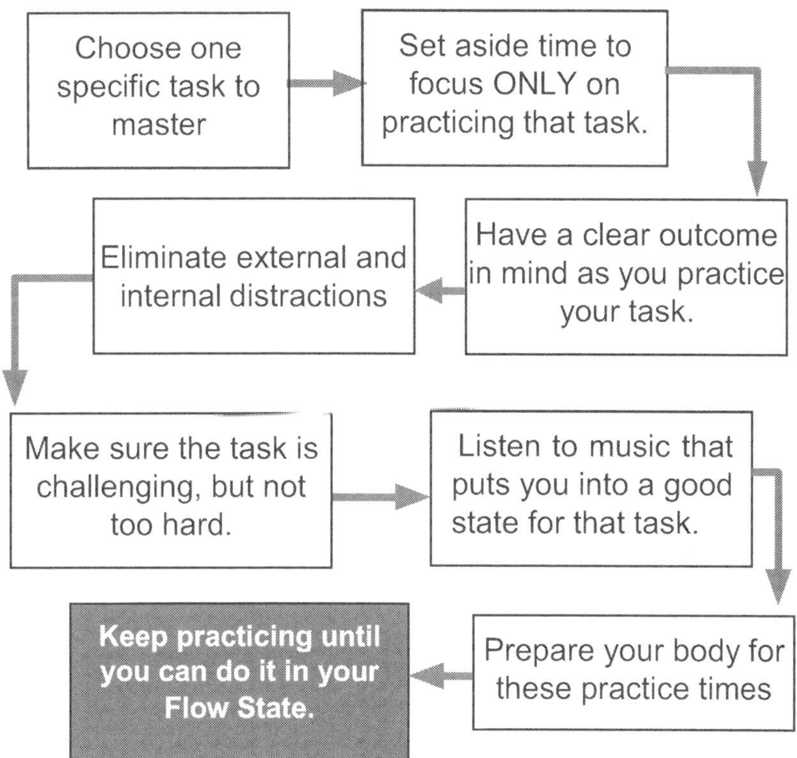

Follow these simple steps above and start to understand your mental states and what triggers them. Most importantly, remember our analogy from the beginning of this section. Your mental state represents how well (or poorly) your self-driving car is running while your mental framework represents your car's navigational software and the data sources it's plugged into. If your mentality is consistently strong and positive but your mental framework (software) is misguided, you'll have a tough time mastering your mental states. But with the right mental framework, managing and mastering the rhythm of your mental states will become second nature.

What's Your Ideal Mental Framework?

What is a mental framework? Think of your thoughts as pictures that you'd put inside a frame to hang on your wall. You can put a picture inside a wooden frame, a metal frame, or a cheap plastic frame. The frame can be white, black, silver, brown, filled with patterns or color gradients. Regardless, the frame in which you put a picture changes the way you perceive the picture itself. Therefore, people buy the most expensive or exquisite frames for their wedding photos.

Thoughts, ideas, and experiences can be "set" into mental frames in the same way, dramatically changing how we see the world and ourselves. For example, if I believe that "all dogs are dangerous," I have set the concept of "dogs" into my "dangerous" frame. This changes how I experience and react to dogs. If I walk into my friend's house and her dog runs up to me, my brain not only fires up my neural network that recognizes and responds to dogs, but also sends a signal to my amygdala, which detects threats to my safety. That signal shoots down my spinal column, activating glands to release "fight or flight" hormones into my bloodstream. My body prepares me to fight the dog or to run from it. I can try to manage this using mental exercises, positive affirmations, and other superficial techniques. But if my mental framework doesn't change, I'll never lose my fear of dogs. This is an example of the perception shaping progression of mental frameworks.

This is the power of mental frameworks and how they shape our life:

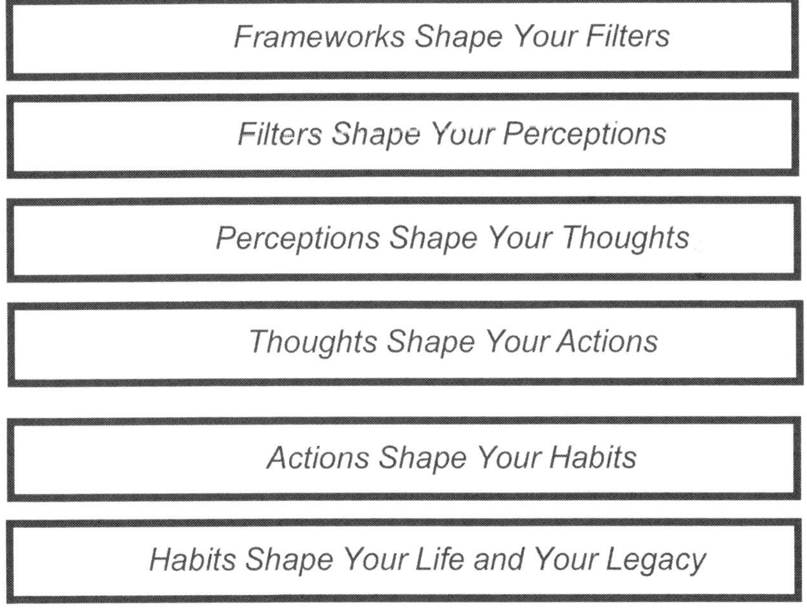

The "filters" represent how your brain decides what to pay attention to and what to ignore. Effective mental filters will filter out worthless information and information that disempowers you or hinders your performance. They will also help you recognize opportunities where most people only see obstacles, and guide your perceptions to seek out opportunities, while shaking off the distractions. Once you perceive the world this way, your thoughts will align toward your highest ideals and influence your actions. Over time, actions become habits and habits will come to shape your life.

The science behind this is rock solid. Cognitive linguists have conducted experiments that prove how our mental frameworks shape the way we think about things that are experientially unrelated. In one experiment, the participants walked into a building and were greeted by someone who immediately handed them a drink, asking them to hold it. Half of the participants were handed a cold drink, like soda or iced tea. The other half were handed a warm drink like coffee or hot tea. After the experiment was over, all the participants were asked to evaluate the overall friendliness of the person who greeted them.

Nothing was asked or mentioned about the drink. Nevertheless, most participants greeted by someone with a cold drink described their host as unfriendly whereas those greeted with a warm drink described their host as friendly. Why? Because in the English language, unfriendly people and situations are generally referred as "cold" or "icy" while friendly people are described as warm. This is an example of how a common, rarely-thought-about mental framework literally causes us to experience the world differently than it really is. Many other experiments and variations of this have been conducted proving that our framing of things determines how we perceive and experience them in the real world.

This is why I compared your mental frameworks to the navigational software in a self-driving car. The same metaphor applies to ***any*** data-driven appliance in the Internet of Things. Each appliance's performance in this global network depends on the quality of its data source and data processing software. The key difference is that what's happening inside your brain and nervous system is much more complex than this.

This is the power of a mental framework and its ability to shape, distort, or change our real-world experiences. In some cases, our mental frameworks are helpful. For instance, if your brain has set screeching tires behind you in the "danger" frame, that's a good thing. But other mental frameworks cause us to develop irrational fears and self-sabotaging habits that end up deeply embedded into our mental architecture. Before we talk about how to recognize and reframe these mental frameworks, let me give you one more example of how our frameworks can literally pit one side of our brain against the other.

Dr. Michael S. Gazzaniga is one of the world's leaders on the difference between the right brain and left brain. Dr. Gazzaniga has conducted some amazing experiments which demonstrate that our right and left brain can behave almost like two different people. In case you're unfamiliar, your brain has two halves, or hemispheres. The left brain dominates speech, language, and analytical problem solving. It thinks in language. The right brain dominates visual motor tasks and thinks in pictures. These two halves communicate with one another through the "Corpus Callosum." This communication can be severed through a medical procedure called a "corpus callosotomy." The operation was meant to treat seizures, but also gave scientists like Michael S. Gazzaniga the opportunity to conduct experiments on each side of the brain independently and to compare the results. In one experiment, the right and left brains were shown a series of separate pictures. Both halves were then asked to choose an item from a list of options that best fitted the picture they saw. The left hand (controlled by the right brain) pointed to the right brain's choice, while the right hand (controlled by the left brain) pointed to the left brain's choice. When the patient was asked why the right brain chose what it did, only the speech-controlling left brain could answer. But since the patient's left brain was unable to communicate with the right brain, it simply made up a story about the right brain's choice.

For example, in one case, the right half saw a snow scene, while the left half saw a chicken foot. The right brain chose a snow shovel, which makes sense. But, when the left brain was asked about the choice, it looked at the chicken foot and said that the right brain had chosen that because the shovel was supposed to clean out the chicken's coup. In other words, instead of saying "I don't know," the left brain rationalized and reframed the right brain's decision by making up a story out of thin air.

Think about what this means in terms of your mental frameworks. In a normal person, the right and left brain can communicate with one another. But this experiment proves that the "talking" part of our mind has no problem making up stories about why we make the choices we do. It has no problem reframing things and therefore literally changes our understanding of something based on explanations which might not even be true or relevant. This is how people with negative mental frameworks develop excuses about why they do what they do. They are associating things that have nothing to do with one another. Their brain is perceiving the world based on those associations and their "thinking" mind (left brain) is making up lies to rationalize their bad decisions. This is how ***all*** brains are wired and we can't overcome this by simply "changing the way we think." We must detect and alter our negative mental frameworks and replace them with positive ones. This is where one of the most important brain fuels comes into play[ix].

Self-Awareness: The Master Key to Reliable Mental Frameworks

Self-awareness has quickly surfaced as one of the most important qualities in business and in building relationships. If you have minimal self-awareness, you won't know what's driving your behaviors. Therefore, you'll have a hard time being consistent in your performance. For many, self-awareness is the critical factor in assessing their assumptions about their own capabilities and skill sets. In fact, psychologists speak of something called the Dunning Kruger Effect, which states that people who are incompetent at a particular task typically have an overinflated sense of their competence. In Layman's speech, they're too incompetent to realize how incompetent they are and might even think they're great at something that they are most certainly not. People who lack awareness are not good in sales or leadership roles. They have a hard time self-correcting or improving their performance because they literally can't see their own shortcomings.

Self-awareness starts with understanding your past, present, and future in full context. In return, those lacking self-awareness end up stuck in failures and regrets over their past or in the dreams of their future, while getting barely anything accomplished in the present. Self-aware individuals know how to live in the present because they know that it's the only time in which they can truly live, work, and grow.

Psychologist Endel Tulving coined the word autonoetic, which is the ability to know where you are in time. This might sound too obvious to be worth mentioning, but our imaginations give us the ability to wander into the past and future, both when we are with others and by ourselves. Sometimes this is a good thing, such as when you're practicing visualization. But in many cases, we misuse this ability and get lost in our thoughts of the past or the future. Real self-awareness is about understanding yourself as who you really are in the present, not who you imagine yourself to be or remember yourself to have been.

How well do you know your "present self?" Think about it in terms of this simple calculation. Consider...

The percentage of time you spend focused on the past.

The percentage of time you spend focused on the future.

The percentage of time you spend focused on the present.

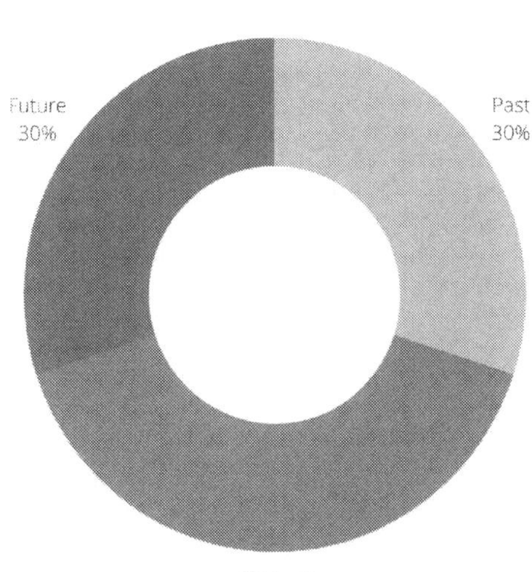

For example, you might be spending 30% of your time focused on who you were and events of the past, 30% of your time focused on who you hope to be in your future and only 40% of your time focused on who you're *truly being* in the present. Yet, the present is the only time frame in which you can make an impact. True, your past can help you learn from mistakes so that you can be more effective in the present. True, your future can inspire you with hope and direction for bringing the best of who you are into the present moment. But how well can you really understand yourself when you spend only a sliver of your time living in the present?

Now is the only time you can act, and it's your actions that reveal who you truly are and what you're truly capable of. Sure, you can build an idealized image of yourself based on some imagined future. You can also build an insecure or incomplete picture of yourself based on your past missteps, or an outdated view of yourself based on what you've previously done.

Genuine self-awareness allows you to get an honest grasp on where your mental frameworks are steering your life. Most importantly, you must be present with others if you hope to build healthy personal and professional relationships and to become a leader. So, put yourself through a personal assessment and make sure that most of your time is focused on thriving in the present.

There is a time to reflect on the past and tap into your future visions. But this should be done during visualization practices. If you take care of this in your private time and be present when you're with others or working on a task, your ability to focus, to work hard, to communicate well, to build relationships, and to influence others will become masterful. Finally, living in the present also expands your self-awareness because you'll see yourself in the context of the here and the now.

The more you grow, the more you'll discover that self-awareness is your compass and that it's essential for fueling your true capabilities. Being able to consistently assess and measure where you are is pivotal to raising the bar and pushing beyond your limitations. Most importantly, it will help you recognize your mental frameworks and how they're affecting you. This self-directed clarity is even more important than having clarity about where you want to be in life.

Brendon Burchard opens his High Performing Habits book with what I think is the most important element as you navigate your personal path in life: ***clarity***. I'm not just talking about the clarity of what you want. Plenty of people are already talking about that. Burchard was talking about clarity in yourself, your skills, your social well-being, and your service to others. Maintaining and focusing on this clarity package will arm you with the skills to make quality decisions about your future. Fueling yourself with habits that will provide clarity and increased self-awareness, will maximize your capability development. You can start by practicing self-awareness about your mental state, and your mental frameworks today. That said, our next step is to unpack how your mental frameworks can either support or hinder each of your Five Prime Capabilities.

Mental Frameworks for Developing Confidence

What are your mental frameworks about confidence? Are they fueling your Flow State or holding you back from pursuing an uneasy, but more fruitful journey? It's easy to fool ourselves with platitudes about this, so let's really give it some thought. Think about the encounters you've had with confident people. Were these encounters positive, or do you feel these confident people took advantage of you? When you meet a confident person, do you immediately find yourself looking for their approval? Do you act subservient to them in some way?

More importantly, think of all the times in your life when your confidence got you into trouble. Think about the times you've been confident, and some envious person has accused you of being arrogant. All of these are examples of how the concept of confidence might get set into negative frames.

For example, if seemingly confident people have manipulated or mistreated you, your mind might have framed confident people as being untrustworthy or opportunistic. This means that every time you think of yourself as confident, you raise the subconscious fear or worry that people might see ***you*** as untrustworthy or opportunistic, which makes your subconscious mind uneasy. Psychologists call this inner conflict "cognitive dissonance." Cognitive dissonance is that uneasy, anxious feeling you get when trying to entertain an idea that clashes with one of your existing core beliefs. In some cases, this uneasiness is useful as it acts almost like your second conscience. After all, if I feel uneasy when I see someone beating a dog, that's cognitive dissonance telling me that what they're doing is morally wrong. Other times, however, cognitive dissonance keeps us trapped by our beliefs about what is and is not possible, or what we do and don't deserve. For example, if you see confident people as opportunistic or arrogant, trying to see yourself as a confident person will create an internal conflict. If this conflict persists, it will put you in the fight or flight mental state for longer periods of time than you should be. In time, your subconscious mind will start looking for ways to restore equilibrium. Sound familiar? It should. We discussed it a few pages back when we talked about brain waves and your mental states. This is how your mental frameworks can get in the way of you growing into your best self. Again, it goes back to our progression.

1. Frameworks shape your filters.
2. Filters shape your perceptions.
3. Perceptions shape your thoughts.
4. Thoughts shape your actions.
5. Actions shape your habits.
6. Habits shape your life and your legacy.

Confidence Frameworks

Now let's check out a list of common negative frameworks regarding confidence, and a positive alternatives for each…

Negative Framework #1:

"Confident people are opportunistic and selfish."

Positive Framework #1:

"My confidence makes me a better person."

Negative Framework #2:

"Confident people are authorities over me."

Positive Framework #2:

"Confident people are still my equals."

Negative Framework #3:

"My confidence will make people envious of me."

Positive Framework #3:

"My confidence isn't subject to people's approval."

Negative Framework #4:

"My confidence to try new things led me into very uncomfortable territory."

Positive Framework #4:

"My confidence to try new things has helped me learn

new things and overcome unnecessary fears."

Negative Framework #5:

"I shouldn't be confident if I've just failed at something."

Positive Framework #5:

"My confidence isn't subject to my performance."

Negative Framework #6:

"I can't be confident until I've earned it."

Positive Framework #6:

"My confidence isn't attached to the outcome. It's a tool for shaping my future."

The last few examples are the most important since they deal with one of the most common enemies of self-confidence: rigid perfectionism. Confidence steers go-getters toward challenges with a mindset geared to achieve success by learning from their failures, reapplying themselves, and "leveling up" their performance. Those who fear failure become too intimidated to even try. They never move off the starting line to pursue things that are out of their comfort zone.

It's important to remember that confidence isn't about feeling comfortable. It's about believing in your ability to figure things out, while at peace with yourself, even in the face of discomfort, adversity, or failure. People aren't just born with confidence. They build it over the course of their lives. Over time, our confidence (or lack of it) determines our outcomes and our ability to persevere in the face of failure.

But demanding perfection from yourself ensures that you'll lose confidence as you grow older. In time, you'll stop challenging yourself to try new things and end up a shell of who you could be.

The harsh reality about failure and confidence is that failure is inevitable so long you're pursuing new things. People who frame confidence as consistent perfection can't handle this. When their failures are big enough, they come to see those failures as a reflection of who they are. This is painful. In time, people throw in the towel and settle for something more reasonable, just to escape this pain. It is an epidemic that sabotages many first-time entrepreneurs. The pain or the anxiety of financial instability forces them to make decisions which will (hopefully) alleviate the pain. In other words, they give up and settle for a job that restores comfort and stability. I'm not saying this isn't an important stepping stone, but the comfort of the steady paycheck can be the component that keeps them focused on comfort instead of confidence.

Of course, confidence is important for more than just salespeople, entrepreneurs, and people in executive positions. Confidence is also important in sports, the performing arts, dating, meeting new people, and many other life ambitions. This makes unwavering confidence a skill that you must master, and it starts with your mental frameworks. When your mental frameworks are optimized for maximum confidence, your sense of self-worth becomes invincible.

What are your mental frameworks about confidence?

Stop for a moment and write down all the things you associate high confidence with, both in yourself and in others.

What are your memories about confident people?

How about the moments in your life when you were confident?

How are these past experiences shaping your mental frameworks about confidence?

Are these frameworks fueling your confidence, or draining it?

How can you replace these negative frameworks with positive ones?

Take a minute to assess your mental frameworks about confidence, and see how your "Mental Navigational Software" might be influencing you to make wrong turns in your life.

Mental Frameworks for Developing Adaptability

The principles we just talked about also apply to your mental frameworks regarding adaptability. Change is inevitable. Your ability to step into new and challenging environments with people that may not share the same values and perspectives as you, and handle it with calm and fortitude, is a skill that is developed.

In addition, throughout your adaptability framework journey it is imperative that you understand a very strange aspect of the human mind that fools much of our world in many ways, cognitive bias, or confirmation bias. Confirmation bias is searching for or interpreting information in a way that confirms one's preconceptions or beliefs. Some refer to this as the "herd effect". Our mind has a weird way of wanting to confirm ideas that we perceive, based on prior, established beliefs. It can literally trick us into strengthening our belief in something, just because we already believe or see it in some given way. This is why it's important to understand this trap that our minds can play on ourselves and to understand how to maintain logical thinking throughout our journey of perceiving the world. Your ability to develop an adaptable mental framework, starts with your ability to understand and implement logical thinking, while avoiding confirmation biases that can misguide you along the way.

For example, let's say you have an idea that you think has a lot of merit in the world. As you discuss the idea with friends and family, they also agree it's a good idea. Your ability to stress test your idea with others that challenge the idea's viability is your ability to work against this mysterious cognitive bias that exist. If you only continue talking to your small circle around you that believes in your idea without seeking challenging logic, you can easily get stuck in confirmation bias that can blind your ability to perceive necessary information maximize critical thinking.

Building an adaptable framework starts with understanding how our minds naturally work to conserve energy by not being adaptable. Our minds have a mysterious way of wanting to confirm our already preconceived beliefs.

So, let's get right to the list of common frameworks and their positive alternatives...

Adaptability Frameworks

Negative Framework #1:

"This is the way I've always done it."

Positive Framework #1:

"I'll learn and grow more by trying different approaches."

Negative Framework #2:

"If it's not broken, don't fix it."

Positive Framework #2:

"You don't have to be sick to get better."

Negative Framework #3:

"People will laugh at my ideas."

Positive Framework #3:

"The best ideas in history were often laughed at."

Negative Framework #4:

"Trying new things makes me uncomfortable."

Positive Framework #4:

"Failing is part of the journey."

Negative Framework #5:

"Adapting means compromising my values."

Positive Framework #5:

"I can try new methods, without changing my core principles."

Negative Framework #6:

"Adapting might lead to failure."

Positive Framework #6:

"Failure to adapt will eventually make my skills and experience irrelevant."

What are your memories about being adaptable or dealing with adaptable people?

How about the moments in your life when you tried something new or creative?

How are these past experiences shaping your mental frameworks about adaptability?

Are these frameworks fueling your adaptability or draining it?

How can you replace your negative adaptability frameworks with positive ones?

Mental Frameworks for Developing Resilience

Again, the same principles apply to your mental frameworks regarding resilience. How do you handle rejection, defeat and failures is critical to your ability to maximize forward progressions? Installing effective frameworks for how to deal with these, is the process to evolving throughout your journey.

So here are some common frameworks and their alternatives.

Resilience Frameworks

Negative Framework #1:

"I don't have time to rest and recover. I need to work now."

Positive Framework #1:

"Resting IS work. When I rest, my body is hard at work recovering my mental and physical faculties."

Negative Framework #2:

"I've already tried and failed at that"

Positive Framework #2:

"I'm more prepared for my second opportunity"

Negative Framework #3:

"What if I embarrass myself?"

Positive Framework #3:

"My results are not my identity"

Negative Framework #4:

"I'm not resilient"

Positive Framework #4:

"Resilience starts with a choice"

What are your memories about being resilient or dealing with tough, resilient people?

How about the moments in your life when you recovered quickly from something?

Are any frameworks fueling your resilience or draining it?

How can you replace these negative resilient frameworks with positive ones?

Mental Frameworks for Developing Focus

Focused people are easy to admire and to envy. Most of us have known at least one person with a near superhuman ability to focus all their attention and energy on a single ambition -- often at the expense of other things. While balance is important, it's equally important that you have a central focus for your life and that you work hard at it until you succeed. Ordinary people never learn to do this, and often because they have negative or erroneous mental frameworks about focused people.

Here are some common examples and their positive alternatives.

FOCUS FRAMEWORKS

Negative Framework #1:

"Focused people are selfish."

Positive Framework #1:

"Focused people don't waste time."

Negative Framework #2:

"I get distracted easily."

Positive Framework #2:

"Focus must be developed and I'm in control of that."

Negative Framework #3:

"If I focus on just one thing, I'll miss out on other opportunities."

Positive Framework #3:

"People who try to do too much end up doing very little."

Negative Framework #4:

"Too much focus is obsession, and obsession is unhealthy."

Positive Framework #4:

"Learning to get obsessed with something can be my superpower."

Negative Framework #5:

"I have to answer this email (phone call, etc.) right now."

Positive Framework #5:

"I won't sacrifice long term value for short term urgency."

Negative Framework #6:

"I do better multitasking."

Positive Framework #6:

"Multitasking fools my brain into thinking that I'm getting more done than I really am."

I know most people consider multitasking to be a good thing, so positive framework #6 demands an explanation. When you're multitasking, your brain gives you a "reward" by releasing dopamine (your reward hormone) every time you switch from one thing to another. This fools your brain into thinking it's getting more done than it really is. Numerous studies have proven that people who are distracted by multitasking are less productive than people who are focused on a single task. In fact, one famous example is the study that showed why people high on drugs did better on aptitude tests than people who were juggling multiple tasks while taking the test. So, if your mental framework confuses multitasking with productivity, that's a framework you'll want to ***focus*** on[x].

What are your memories about being focused or dealing with focused and ambitious people?

How about the moments in your life when you were *really* focused on something?

How are these past experiences shaping your mental frameworks about being focused?

Are these frameworks fueling your ability to focus or draining it?

How can you replace any negative focus frameworks with positive ones?

Mental Frameworks for Leadership Development

Leadership standards are evolving almost as quickly as technology. The spotlight and expectations placed on leaders today is essential for organizational and social impact. Understanding your own frameworks while gaining awareness into how to build ideal leadership frameworks, is one of your most critical opportunities to leading and impacting others throughout your journey.

LEADERSHIP FRAMEWORKS

Negative Framework #1:

"Leaders tell people what to do."

Positive Framework #1:

"Real leaders lead by example and inspire people."

Negative Framework #2:

"Leaders get more privileges."

Positive Framework #2:

"Leaders have more responsibilities."

Negative Framework #3:

"I haven't been given a leadership role."

Positive Framework #3:

"Many leaders have to become leaders before they're recognized as such."

Negative Framework #4:

"Leaders should always know what to do."

Positive Framework #4:

"A real leader knows when to defer to someone else's expertise or direction."

Negative Framework #5:

"I don't want to step on someone's toes."

Positive Framework #5:

"Leaders take bold action, followers play it safe."

Negative Framework #6:

"I'm not likeable enough to be a leader."

Positive Framework #6:

"Real leadership is grounded in principles, not personalities."

Negative Framework #7:

"No one will give me a chance to lead."

Positive Framework #7:

"Leaders don't wait for chances, they create them."

Negative Framework #8:

"I'm the leader, so people should do what I say."

Positive Framework #8:

"Leadership isn't about roles or titles, it's about competence, character, and service."

What are your memories about leaders -- the people themselves and the experience of being led by them?

How about the moments in your life when you were *really* sure of yourself and others believed in you?

Were people jealous or threatened by you?

How are these past experiences shaping your mental frameworks regarding leadership?

Are these frameworks fueling your natural ability to lead or draining it?

What leadership frameworks are you missing from your toolbox?

Now that we've covered these common frameworks, let's look at three Master Frameworks that, once embraced, will "trickle down" to fuel all your mental frameworks, wash out your negative ones, and replace them with positive frameworks.

Master Framework #1: The Self-Image Framework

If I had to pick one Self-Image Framework to install into all my readers' brains, it would be the "Growth Mindset." On the flip side of this is a mindset that wants to maintain things as they are and sees any attempt to change the status quo as a threat —the "Fixed Mindset."

Wallace Wattles calls these two conflicting mindsets the "Creative Mindset" and the "Competitive Mindset." While I believe that competition is more often healthy than toxic, anyone who has read Wattles' book *The Science of Getting Rich* will realize that the competition he talked about was based on fear and envy. I also believe the "Fixed Mindset" is the product of fear-based or complacent thinking and a need for self-preservation at the expense of progress. The more time you spend cultivating a Growth Mindset, the more fuel you'll give to your Five Prime Capabilities, the more momentum you'll gain.

Of course, it's rare that our life is dominated by the Growth Mindset or the Fixed Mindset. More often, people are torn between the two, living at times in one, and other times in the other. Such people don't typically even control when or why they switch from one of these mindsets to the other. It's purely reactionary.

Those who spend most of their time in the Fixed Mindset minimize their ability to adapt and lead. When you have a growth-focused self-image, however, you see everything as an opportunity to grow. Your creative problem solving is activated, your brain is healthy and strong, and your ability to retain and to apply your knowledge is dramatically magnified. Most importantly, you'll have the confidence to face challenges with clarity and courage. This point is vital because how our brain processes challenges determines whether we live with a Growth Mindset or a Fixed Mindset.

There is also a Survival Mindset that presents itself and can trigger our fight or flight chemicals in our body. If you see a threat to either your established patterns, or your idealized daydreams, your body can trigger this fight or flight response. When you enter this state, your body shuts down your higher brain function and the organs involved in digestion and recovery so that it can prioritize that energy toward fighting the threat.

If you want an example of how toxic the Survival Mindset is, just look at how divisive political discourse has become in the United States. Nearly every campaign message is designed to frame us as victims, and our "opponents" as victimizers. Victim thinking is a black hole that traps you in the Survival Mindset. It forces you to see everyone as either prey or predator. Their objective in passing fear and transitioning your physiological state into a Survival Mindset is literally part of people's daily strategy. Your ability to process and filter these emotionally driven messages, while not reacting on your immediate impulses, is part of your framework journey toward a better life.

True, we live in a world that has power structures in place creating not-so-powerful situations for us sometimes. It's easy to fall into the victim's mindset and feel you need to fight for survival. Certain environments and upbringings can magnify this temptation. Survival is also necessary, making it more tempting to live out of the survival mindset. But living in a Survival Mindset can trap you in a fear focused reality. It will erode your quality of life, your potential, and your spirit. But you can choose to be proactive instead of reactive. You can choose Growth over Survival, and love over fear.

If you see every challenge as an opportunity to grow, it completely changes your physiological response to adversity, to change, and to things that challenge your worldview. This has a dramatic impact on your confidence, your adaptability, your resilience, your ability to focus, and your ability to understand and lead others. It also makes you more resilient to stress. If you can learn to master stress, your capabilities will be at their full capacity, even under pressure, giving you an edge over people who can't deliver under pressure. If you haven't developed this stress management muscle, you will be more prone to making irrational and impulsive decisions just to relieve the stress.

Are you starting to see how important your self-image framework is, and why it's so important to have one that's based on growth, rather than survival, perfection, or preservation of what's familiar? Whatever emotional sabotage you've used against yourself or your capabilities, you've got to take a step back, breathe, and realize that you have control over your mental frameworks. You might not have complete control over the results of your life, or even your feelings yet, but you do have control over your mental framework regarding yourself and what you're capable of. The right self-image will empower you to do this so that you can outgrow your insecurities and develop your Five Prime Capabilities. You can only develop these capabilities in a Growth Mindset.

Master Framework #2: Your Economic Worldview

For years, we've thought of productivity as the most economically significant skill. This isn't entirely true anymore.

Productivity and knowledge were the economic superpowers of the industrial age whereas our society is evolving rapidly. Your ability to earn and to advance in the workplace depended mostly on your ability to apply your knowledge to get things done, or by applying your knowledge to get other to get things done. Today, the new economic superpowers are innovation and adaptability.

Knowledge is everywhere these days. Any motivated individual can get their hands on very specialized knowledge, but it takes wisdom to discern good knowledge from bad and it takes creativity to apply that knowledge in a way that creates unique value in the New Economy. More people are starting to realize this, but many have remained stuck in the industrial age model. Sadly, a lot of people still assume creativity to be something you either "have" or "don't have." That's not true. Creativity is something you *do*. The same is true with many of the other capabilities we talk about in this book. This means that creativity can be learned by practice.

Leaders today are expected to be empathetic, intuitive, and creative. These are all right brain qualities and the more you exercise and fuel your right brain, the better you'll get at them. How do you accomplish this? Check out the section above on mental states, and the sections on your frameworks regarding adaptability, focus, and leadership. Most importantly, start doing something to reawaken your childlike creative qualities. The great artist Pablo Picasso said *"It takes a very long time to become young."*

Growing up is inevitable in many ways, but you shouldn't lose the sense of wonder and curiosity you see in young children. If you have lost it, use your mental state practice time to work on getting it back. When you were a child, the world was your oyster. You dreamed of achieving great things. You looked up to people and always sought information and new experiences. Most people lose this sense of learning as they age, thinking that they know everything already. I suspect a lot of this has to do with our assumptions that the economic superpowers of the industrial age are still as dominant in the New Economy as they were in the Old Economy. But they're not.

When you shut down your creative imagination, your mind stops learning and developing. It stops generating new ideas for the same reason people who are bedridden for years lose the strength to walk. A Survival Mindset also closes off this ability to be creative by putting you in a fight or flight state, instead of a calm and adaptable one. Your ability to increase your creative thinking is directly connected to your ability to solve problems most effectively.

This does not mean that productivity is not still an important skill. Being productive is still extremely important but your ability to innovate and use creative thinking in the marketplace is becoming even more essential every day to survive and thrive.

What are your mental frameworks about what it takes to become and to remain economically viable in today's marketplace?

Are these frameworks fueling your creativity, or draining it?

What's your ideal mental state for generating creative ideas?

How adaptable and comfortable are you in unique settings? Are you capable of making the most of the situation and the people involved, or clamming up and desiring comfort?

****

One of the best traits you can acquire and maintain is curiosity. If you're curious or inquisitive, you'll continue to seek knowledge and understanding. There's an overwhelming amount of information in the world, and not all of it is good. So, unless you think critically, you will either follow false information, or you'll hold yourself back from maximizing your knowledge. They say the average CEO reads 50 books a year. Not everyone wants to be a CEO, but there's always a price to pay if you want to accomplish great things. As a CEO it's extremely important that you're well-rounded in your knowledge so that you can guide your company with as much awareness as possible. Having the ability to connect ideas to solutions is one of the most important skills a CEO can develop. People look up to their CEO for answers to their problems. The CEO is expected to make swift, consistent and effective decisions that will lead their organization and inspire their people. Their ability to stay curious and focused on learning is one of the most important ingredients to his/her success. However, this is also true of parents, mentors, and everyone else in leadership roles. This is why curiosity is an essential skill for the New Economy.

****

Master Framework #3: Your Relationship Framework

A healthy relationship framework causes you to treat your relationships more like organic lifeforms than contractual agreements. Such a framework is based on empathy, service, and leading by example, not by manipulation. Few people realize that normally functioning brains are literally wired for this kind of worldview. For example, when you see someone experiencing an emotion, your brain fires up a network of what neuroscientists call "mirror neurons." These neurons cause our internal experience to "mirror" the experience of someone we're observing. For example, that sympathetic feeling that you get when you see someone crying. That's coming from your mirror neurons reflecting the other person's experience inside your brain. The same is true when we see someone explode in anger at us. Our brain mirrors that experience, and we respond to their anger by getting angry ourselves.

Therefore, having self-awareness and being present is critical for relating with others. Once you accept that your brain is firing those mirror neurons for the sake of creating empathy for the other person, you can make a better choice about how to respond to their emotions. The opposite of this mental framework is the one saying "I'll give you back as good (or as bad) as you gave me."

People with this transactional worldview never grow beyond the people they surround themselves with, because they're too busy mirroring the emotions of other people. They also never learn to become a leader, because they don't know when to generate their own decisions, and when to defer to other people. This later statement might sound counterintuitive. However, being a good leader requires that you know when to defer to someone else's expertise or even to their leadership. For example, suppose I hired a marketing director for my company. I disagree with her on how to promote a new product. Do I let her take the lead, or do we do it my way because I'm her boss? If I trust my own judgment in hiring her, I'll lead by deferring to her expertise. But this is only possible if my relationship framework is based on empathy, service, and leading by example, not manipulation.

This is how you gain the trust and respect from those around you. This is how you develop the soft skills of good negotiation, empathetic listening, and smart delegation. These skills are helpful in most things you do. This mental framework is also the foundation for mastering the now famous "Emotional Intelligence," which is one of the key skills of the New Economy. People not embracing this framework will wear out their relationships the same way they wear out the tires on their car. Their past will be strewn with the wreckage of disbanded friendships, and/or estranged partnerships, none of which they held onto for long. But, when we start treating relationships like living things, we form connections that are built to last.

Now that we've covered all the bases on mental frameworks, let's deal with the most common objection to changing our brain.

"Can I Really Change My Mindset?"

Yes, you can, and to believe otherwise is the most crippling mental framework. But before we talk about how you can really change your mindset, let's clarify the differences between mindsets and mental frameworks first, as people tend to confuse the two with each other. In short, your mindset is the *combination* of your mental state and your mental frameworks.

Once again, you most definitely can change and evolve your mindset. Our brains are malleable. Neuroscientists call this innate ability "neuroplasticity." In *The Brain that Changes Itself*, Norman Doidge lays out several miraculous cases of neuroplasticity at work. In one story, a woman born with only half a brain developed the ability to think more effectively than many people with a full brain. In other stories, stroke victims have regained the ability to speak using neuroplasticity. There are even more cases documented by neuroscientists and more "miracles" are happening every day. That should tell you that you *can* change your neuro-associations to support a healthier mindset. This is done with the mental state exercises we talked about earlier, through applying self-awareness to recognize your negative mental frameworks, and by visualization, which we'll discuss soon.

The more you practice, the more you can fuel your brain for optimal confidence, adaptability, resilience, focus, and leadership. You'll also develop the ability to generate ideas, solve problems, and master skills beyond the scope of this book. Eventually, you will create new growth in your mind.

Developing your mind also empowers you to embrace the three Master Frameworks. These frameworks might just lead you to your million-dollar idea you've been dreaming about. The most ambitious and productive people in history are overwhelmingly obsessed with learning. They continue to develop their brain and its ability to generate ideas that provide immense value for others. On the other hand, people who stop using their motor and learning skills are more vulnerable to dementia, according to recent scientific and psychological studies[xi].

To fuel your Five Prime Capabilities, dump the assumption that people were born with tendencies toward negative frameworks and there is no way to change it, because science has told us otherwise. It has told us that our minds are malleable, and they change depending on what we focus on throughout our journey. They also change with or without our direction. Therefore, a better question is whether this change will fuel your capabilities or cause them to atrophy. Your mind is flexible, but you must continue to grow it with intention. As you continue to stretch your mind and develop new skills, your potential capabilities become your realized capabilities and you discover new levels of potential you never knew you were capable of.

Sadly, some people stop changing their habits and pushing their minds at a certain age. They stop learning regardless of how much momentum they have built up. Eventually, the stagnation catches up with them and they fail to advance in life. Soon, they'd realize they've lost their momentum. By that time, they are often too tired to make the changes needed to restore their prior glory. On the other hand, people who embrace the power and flexibility of their brain continue to learn and grow late into life, and many of them make their greatest contributions to the world at a stage where other people have already thrown in the towel.

My guess is you'd rather be one that continues to bring value till the end. So, let's wrap up the Brain Fuel section with the skill that combines your mental state and your mental frameworks to maximize your mindset. Let's send your capabilities into 5th gear with ***visualization***.

Visualization: How Mindsets Are Made

Visualization is the single most powerful habit that will fuel and synchronize your mental frameworks and your mental states. Visualization is disciplined daydreaming and highly intentional. Instead of randomly imaging pleasant scenarios, you intentionally determine *what* you "dream about" based on what you want to obtain, achieve, or experience. In other words, you "get down" with your Primary Intention during visualization practice.

The Benefits of Visualization

Visualization programs your consciousness to seek out ideas, connections, and opportunities that will help you achieve your Primary Intention.

Visualization primes your subconscious to come up with creative ideas or inspirations for achieving your Primary Intention.

Visualization "upgrades" your mental state so people with

a similar mindset will want to help you or introduce you to people who can help.

Visualization fuels your confidence, adaptability, resilience, focus, and leadership capabilities with the motivation to pursue your Primary Intention even when you are under pressure.

Visualization programs your mind, both consciously and subconsciously, to identify mental frameworks that are not aligned with your Primary Intention.

How to Visualize

What will you visualize?

Start with the Primary Intention we talked about in the first chapter. Once you have identified this intention, set time aside to train your mind to vividly imagine your Primary Intention coming true. Then, train your mind to enter the best mental state to involve yourself emotionally in this vision so you fuel your motivation, desire, and creativity to achieve that image. In other words, the visualization practice itself doesn't make your intention a reality. But when it aligns your Primary-Intention-based mental framework with your mental state, visualization practices supercharge all your capabilities toward achieving that Primary Intention.

We will call this your "Disciplined Daydream." For example, if you're a writer whose Primary Intention is to win a Pulitzer Prize, merely writing that goal down is not enough. You must set aside, say, 10 minutes a day to imagine exactly what will happen at the moment when you are awarded the prize. Visualize yourself at an award ceremony giving a winner's speech. Visualize your audience's faces as they look at you, applauding, smiling, laughing at your jokes, or even crying as you share your story. You'll visualize yourself pulling the award out of a sealed envelope, staring at it, and feeling an immense amount of awe and gratitude.

Then, visualize yourself going to the store to pick out a frame for that award. You go home and hang it on your wall. You'd be sitting at your desk working as you periodically stop and smile with pride when you see the reward on the wall. There will be stories on TV or in newspapers about your work that won the prize. You show up for TV or radio interviews. You begin to give speeches at universities. At the beginning of each program, the host would introduce you as "The Winner of the Pulitzer Prize for…"

As you imagine these scenarios, you'll visualize every detail: what you see, hear, smell, and feel during these moments. Then, as you practice visualizing your intention, you'll accomplish two important goals:

- You'll increase your focus on creating the exact mental state you expect to be in when you receive the prize in real life.
- You'll recognize any negative mental frameworks which might stop you from achieving your intention.

The second goal is listed here because once you really start to take your visualization practice seriously, your subconscious mind will serve you all kinds of doubts, fears, and other mental obstacles preventing you from achieving your Primary Intention. Don't judge yourself for these thoughts or feel bad about them. They are normal early. Don't tell yourself you "shouldn't have them," and don't get afraid that they will cloud your vision. Treat them as clues of what you need to change to make your visualization practice more positive and to enhance your mental frameworks. Your subconscious mind is empowering you to get clarity on potential obstacles. So, don't judge it for trying to help.

Finding your Primary Intention begins with two questions:

"What kind of life do I want to live?"

"Who must I become in order to live it?"

The answer to the first question combined with knowledge of what that path will look like, informs the answer to the second. For example, if you want to be a Pulitzer winner, what skills will you have to master? What character traits will you need? How will you need to improve your Five Prime Capabilities? What kind of daily brain fuel will you need to make yourself so good at your craft that people will recognize and want to reward you greatly for it?

As you're thinking about these things, don't stop for a second to wonder how this is all going to happen. The reason you don't have what you want right now is because you haven't welcomed or attracted it into your life. If you already knew how to do so, you'd probably have that already. Take this book for instance. Many people asked, "How do you know how to write a book?" The answer was, "I don't know." How could I? I hadn't written a book yet. But as I studied what other authors did to enhance their writing ability and discipline, I worked effortlessly to adopt a writer's habits and abilities, sacrificing many other things I could have done in that time. I spent a lot of time practicing writing and learning the skills of book organization to make it all flow.

It also required me to figure out how to finish and launch it most effectively. What editors and formatters could I hire to polish my first manuscript? It challenged me to do and think the things I'd never done before, and each time I did something new, I learned something that I didn't know when I started. That's how this works. So, don't assume you have to see the entire staircase to take the first step. People who think this way limit themselves before even getting started. If I didn't start this book because I didn't know how to format a book, you would not be reading this.

Visualization isn't about imagining all the action steps between where you are and where you want to be. It's about imagining where you want to be with such vivid and emotionally charged clarity and energy that your Primary Intention will "color" everything that you think and do until it becomes the central focus of your life. You have the control to welcome what you want into your life, but change doesn't come easily. This is the power of shaping the mind and taking control over where you take your mind. This section has equipped you with the brain fuel to master your mental states and your mental frameworks. Now, it's time to align them for achieving your Primary Intention.

Visualization is the language of the subconscious mind and what Carl Jung calls "the Collective Unconscious." If you're unaware or dubious about the Collective Unconscious, that's okay for now. We'll talk more in-depth about that concept in our Spirit Fuel section later. Until then, you can still do your daily visualization practice. To help you get started, let's revisit the mental state practice tips we talked about earlier and apply them toward your visualization practice.

- Choose one specific intention to focus on.
- Make sure it's something that ***really*** excites you.
- Set aside time to focus *only* on visualizing that intention.
- Have a clear outcome in mind as you practice your visualization.
- Eliminate external and internal distractions.
- Start with your Disciplined Daydream and slowly add details.
- Listen to music that puts you into a good state for visualization.
- Prepare your body for these practice times.
- Write some verbal affirmations and recite them three times daily.
- Keep practicing until you can do this in your Flow State.

As you start doing this, it's important to remember the neuroscience we discussed earlier. First, remember that your brain waves will become more settled as you get better at visualizing your intention and at visualizing in general. Second, remember that your mental frameworks will shape your psychological experience of what you're visualizing. Third, remember that neuroplasticity gives your mind the power and flexibility to reward itself towards visualizing your intention more clearly. Finally, total immersion is the best way to become a master at visualization.

So, here are a few things you can do outside of your visualization practice time:

Build a Vision Board: A vision board is a board that you fill with literal pictures to support your intention. You can cut pictures out of a magazine, print images from the web, take pictures, or get a visual clip of your destination. Paste these onto a small to large board (or tack them on a cork board.) Put the board somewhere you can see it each day. Most importantly, put a picture of yourself somewhere on your vision board. This literally makes your intention a visual framework which includes you as a participant, and your brain will build the neuro-associations that support that framework. Use this vision board as a continuous reminder of why you're getting out of bed motivated each day.

Practice Quieting Your Mind: When you first sit down to do your visualization practice, you probably won't be effective at it. Your mind will dart around and kick its feet like a toddler protesting his bedtime. This is normal, especially if you've never tried to discipline your imagination towards visualizing a specific intention. This is why it's important to practice just quieting your mind so that you can start your visualization from a blank slate. Don't think of this as a waste of time. Remember, you're fueling your brain to harmonize your mental state with your mental frameworks to help welcome this intention into your life. If you master the skill of quieting your mind, you'll have a much easier time filling that quiet mind with the vision of what you want.

Collect Real Experiences: Your visualizations will be more effective if you go out into the real world and collect as many experiences as possible to help with your intention. For example, you might not be able to have the real experience of receiving a reward, walking up to the stage, and making a speech about it. But, you can attend award ceremonies, watch other people give speeches, and visualize yourself on the stage. You can stand on the stage of an empty auditorium and imagine a crowd full of people cheering and applauding. You can record speeches of yourself, and mix applause or laughter into the background. Anything that will help you have experiences that are close to what you're visualizing will help build up the neuro-associations that support those experiences and seek them out.

Take Action: This is the most important step, and very often neglected. As you prepare to put your visualization practices into action, remember that taking action and building momentum with little wins is the greatest component in achieving your goal. Even if you have absolutely no idea how to start working towards your intention, just do what you know. These actions may seem insignificant and might even end up being wrong. That's okay. If you take action and fail, you'll still reassess, reapply yourself and thus learn faster than you would by doing nothing. As you inch closer to your intention, your ability to visualize your path will become supercharged with confidence and clarity. With this will come added motivational fuel to propel you forward towards your desired destination. Use Visualization and Disciplined Daydreaming to help you get there.

CHAPTER 5: BODY FUEL

True enjoyment comes from activity of the mind and exercise of the body; the two are ever united.

- Wilhelm von Humboldt

There is more wisdom in your body than in your deepest philosophy.

-Friedrich Nietzsche

Your brain and body should operate as a single intelligent system that is highly organized. They should work in harmony toward achieving your best life. Oddly, this is a counterintuitive statement — and a controversial one for some. Many consider the brain and the body to be separate. Dozens of personal-growth books focus on changing your life by "changing your thinking," concentrating mainly on mental techniques. However, I want to expand this paradigm by redefining "thinking" as something that happens throughout both your brain and your body, which will open the door to a conversation about "fueling" the body as the intelligent organism that it is.

The mental framework of the industrial age is that our bodies operate more like fuel-burning machines than intelligent organisms. That's why we talk about burning calories, feeling "run down," or being "burned out." When something in our body stops working, we might go to a surgeon who eventually opens us up to fix, replace, or remove the "bad" parts to cure the disease. As a result, we've come to think of some reversible conditions as being permanent, like a machine that broke down and must be replaced.

This is ***not*** what I meant when I talked about fueling your body.

The mental framework that regards the body as a fuel-burning machine is a vestige of the Industrial Age. This framework limits your performance and sabotages your capabilities. Thus, I want to introduce a new metaphor for the body — one that treats it more like a data-driven "smart machine" that has become more popular in today's world, such as self-driving cars, smart phones, or other smart appliances in the Internet of Things.

These modern machines are fueled by trustworthy information as much as they are by reliable and sustainable energy. Furthermore, they operate on complex, data-driven software, and systems which in return determine their operation. Most importantly, smart machines are becoming more connected as they share data to build a global network of abundant information. This information network will soon guide the operation of all smart machines around the world and we need to think about fueling our bodies in similar ways. It is more than a fuel-burning machine. Our body is an extremely complex and intelligent organism and is far more complicated than any machine ever built by human hands.

What is the Body Fuel?

We've already talked about how negative mental frameworks are holding us back from maximizing our Five Prime Capabilities. When I talk about "Body Fuel," I'm talking about fueling your brain and body as if they were both parts of a single thinking organism, instead of treating your body as a separate fuel-burning machine. Living organisms don't just use fuels (food, sunlight, water) as energy. They also use them to grow and regenerate according to their natural genetic blueprint. When living organisms aren't properly fueled, they can't grow to their highest and most natural potential. In return, they become weaker and less resilient. The same is true for your brain and body.

Our body is an entire system of living organisms. Your digestive system contains tens of trillions of microorganisms, including an estimated 1,000 species of known bacteria and uncountable unknown ones. Depending on the statistics you read, that's more organisms than the entire population ever lived throughout human history. Therefore, the real question is if the trillions of cells in your body and the army of microbes in your digestive system are working together or against one another.

With that said, if you stick with the fuel-burning machine paradigm, you will find it much harder to maximize your energy. Think back to the furnace vs. generator analogy we talked about in the first chapter. People who have trouble with their weight talk about their bodies as if they were furnaces that either burned energy too fast or too slow, when in fact your body doesn't "burn" energy — because energy cannot be destroyed. It can only change form. This is more than my philosophical speculation. It's a fundamental law of physics called "the Conservation of Energy." When energy enters your body in the form of food, your body turns it into different things depending on how you're fueling the information processes in both your brain and your body.

Finally, fueling your body means rethinking how you regard thinking itself. When we think about how our brain works, we talk about neurons firing or neural networks being built to form complex thoughts. There are approximately 85 billion neurons in our brain and another 15 billion in the spinal column. However, most of us never talk about the fact that there are also billions of neurons throughout the rest of your body. Think about what this means in terms of achieving your full potential. Those who make constant efforts to manage their thoughts give little or no attention to the thinking that's happening in their body. This is about as hard as paddling a canoe upstream. You might be able to make some progress, but you'll accomplish more sustainable results if you can get all the "thinking" cells of your body to work in harmony. To achieve this synchronization, we must start with understanding how our body can work against your best interests if fueled inappropriately.

Is Your Body at War with Itself?

Similar to how proper Brain Fuel makes you more resilient against self-sabotage, proper Body Fuels make you more resilient against physical illnesses. This idea is simple, yet the "body as a fuel-burning machine" paradigm has fooled many of us into neglecting it. Case in point: as I was writing this, nearly every country in the industrialized world was debating how to revive their economy after the Covid-19 shutdown. That's why I thought it would be appropriate to use the coronavirus as an example of how your body can work against itself to the point of death.

Let's look at how the coronavirus kills its human host, as published on WebMD[xii]:

"Many COVID-19 complications may be caused by a condition known as cytokine release syndrome or a cytokine storm. This is when an infection triggers your immune system to flood your bloodstream with inflammatory proteins called cytokines. They can kill tissue and damage your organs."

This tells us that the responses our immune system gives to the virus can also kill our tissues and damage our organs, as if our body is waging a war against itself. And this is not a novel condition caused only by Covid-19. In fact, our immune system has a natural response to injury or infection called inflammation[xiii], which defends your body against viruses and bacteria and to heal or repair damaged tissues. When was the last time you twisted an ankle or got stung by a wasp? Remember that swelling around the injured area? That is inflammation. If your body couldn't produce an inflammatory response, your wounds would become fatally infected. However, inflammation can also become a chronic condition and build up in places where it's more harmful than helpful.

Physicians have found chronic inflammation to be connected with deadly health problems including heart disease, stroke, arthritis, autoimmune diseases, asthma, allergies, and also serve as a host for other health issues that are known for crippling or killing people in their prime.

The inflammatory proteins are called cytokines. Cytokines are chemical "messengers" released during acute inflammation. They rush nutrients and hormones to the inflamed area to repair the damage or fight off an infection sometimes giving you a sore throat as if you're sick because your body is rushing nutrients to that area to fight the infection. Once the injury or infection is healed or defeated, the acute inflammation subsides. Meanwhile, chronic inflammation doesn't have that healing effect. Instead, it produces a slow and often undetectable inflammation which puts your body in a constant inflammation condition.

Since the inflammatory proteins cytokines can also kill tissues and damage organs, chronic inflammation can lead to long-term illness. However, rarely anybody knows that sometimes this subtle inflammation becomes triggered when your immune system perceives an injury or infection that may not actually exist. When this happens, white blood cells rush to a certain area but have nothing to fight, so they start attacking your healthy tissues instead. And just like that, your immune system has put your body at war with itself.

If this doesn't startle you into action, I suggest doing more reading on this topic, especially about inflammation's role in aging. When you're young, it's easy to fall prey to the mental framework that says, "that will never happen to me." You may have subtle chronic inflammation in your body right now that you don't even know about. Some foods can also cause inflammation in your brain, leading to mood disorders like anxiety, depression, and long-term mental illnesses, including dementia and schizophrenia in extreme cases. These issues happen because your immune system has turned against the healthy tissues in your body. The good news is you can reduce or prevent chronic inflammation through the lifestyle choices we are about to discuss in the upcoming section. But before we get to that, let's talk about the second way your body can wage a war on itself[xiv].

Body Fuel and Your "Second Brain"

Here's a creepy thought… you're never really "alone." You carry a universe of tiny lifeforms inside and on your body everywhere you go and most of them are in your gut. These lifeforms we've just talked about inhabit the microbiome. They are micro-creatures living inside your body and feeding off nutrients from things you eat. Like all other biological lifeforms, your gut microbes have needs and ways of meeting those needs. Remember the last time you woke up in the middle of the night craving sweets or a McDonald's burger? Remember that last time you just ***had*** to have something sugar or carb-loaded and you were almost on autopilot as you drove to this food supplier to fill this need?

And remember how guilty you felt afterwards?

This didn't just happen because you lack self-control or simply couldn't say no to your cravings. It happened because the microbes in your gut made you fulfill their needs. Some of them need grease and fat to survive. Others need sugar. However, they can't whip out their cell phone and send you a text asking you to grab them some junk food from the store or hit the Taco Bell drive-thru at 2 am. Nonetheless, they do have a direct information hotline to your brain —the Vagus Nerve.

Think about your Vagus Nerve as your nervous system's information superhighway. It sends thought impulses from your gut to your brain and vice versa. The microbes in your gut send their own signals by releasing chemicals into your digestive organs or your bloodstream. When these chemicals reach your brain, you get the urge to eat whatever these microbes need to survive.

In some ancient and modern Eastern religions and philosophies, a person's gut is considered one's second brain, or "Hara." These people understood that the human *body* has an independent intelligence long before scientists discovered the existence of microbiomes or the Vagus Nerve. In the modern western world, we use terms like the "subconscious mind" to describe the bodily intelligence and automatic brain processes.

No matter what term you use, plenty of modern science also backs up the ancient wisdom about your body having its own mind. Sadly, some people treat their gut-brain like a trash compactor instead of a second brain. And believe me, those nasty junk-food loving microbes in your gut have no complaints about this abuse. In fact, the "feed us now" chemicals they release can get into your bloodstream and penetrate your blood-brain barrier, and eventually reach your conscious-brain. Fortunately, you can reconstruct your gut microbiome by starving off bad organisms and replacing them with ones that desire a healthier diet like organic whole foods, fruits, and vegetables. Have you ever known someone who eats healthy and seems immune to the irresistible cravings for sugar and junk food? This is not because they have some superhuman willpower, even though they do battle to start and maintain a healthy diet. It's because their gut-brain is working in harmony with the rest of their thought processes.

Are you finally starting to see why fueling your capabilities is more than just changing the way you think? If not, here's one more quote to summarize what we just talked about with the "second brain".

"The relationship between our gut microbiota and cognitive function is mediated by the gut–brain axis, a biochemical communication network that links the central nervous system, which houses the brain and spinal cord, with the enteric nervous system and bacteria in the gut. Via the gut–brain axis, bacterial metabolites travel from the gut to the brain, where they impact cognitive function.[xv]*"*

Now that you know that the health of your gut-brain plays a significant role in how your literal brain performs, if you are having difficulties focusing on the mental state exercises from the Brain Fuel section, or if you're struggling to change your mental frameworks, don't worry. Chances are your body isn't receiving proper fuels and is therefore working against your best intentions. So, be patient. We'll talk about how to turn this around in a moment. But before we can get to that, there is a third and the most mind-blowing fact about how your body influences your thinking.

Rethinking Your Subconscious Mind[xvi]

What role does your subconscious mind play in your life?

Think about how you got to where you are today. What beliefs steered you to your current position? Who helped you develop your beliefs and subconscious? Was it you alone or did other people cast external forces to move you forward? Your answers to these questions will tell you about what's going on with your subconscious mind. Most people don't realize *how* they developed certain subconscious impulses and why they can't change these impulses with mental techniques alone. They live on autopilot from the day they were born to the end of their lives. As they move through their days making decisions, they are unknowingly shaping their futures. However, doesn't it make you wonder what is really happening inside your brain and body as you're going about your routines? You've probably heard that your subconscious mind doesn't *know* the difference between real and unreal events. But what does this mean in practical applications?

How the Subconscious Mind Works

Your subconscious mind responds to both exterior and imagined experiences with similar physiological processes. Thought impulses come from action potentials in your neurons that are all over your body. Therefore, thought impulses can travel from your body to your brain and vice versa. But most people don't know that these impulses only differ in frequency. For example, the thought impulse in response to a paper cut is identical to the one you'd have if your arm were cut off by a chainsaw, only on a different frequency.

These impulses are how your subconscious processes sensory input. As we mentioned earlier, these signals can fire in response to both real and imagined experiences, which is why we covered visualization so early in this book. Your conscious mind might be able to tell you that you're only imagining, but your subconscious mind will respond to visualization the same way it would to the real experience as long as your visualization skills are powerful enough to affect your mental and physiological state.

Moreover, your subconscious mind can make decisions independent from your conscious mind's input. For example, some nerve impulses may initiate in your body in response to certain sensory stimuli and travel directly to another place without ever going through the brain. These impulses respond to the stimuli without involving your conscious mind at all. Think about what happens when you touch a hot stove by accident. You yank your hand back instantly without thinking. We call these impulsive habits "reflexes.[xvii]" Some reflexes are wired from birth, whereas others can be developed through repeated experiences, actions, and thoughts like how we become fluent in a foreign language. These developed reflexes are called "conditioned reflexes." They are also known as muscle memories. Like your mental frameworks, your muscle memory can be helpful or harmful to your success. To use the same example, when you accidently touch something hot, your hand jerks back instantly before your brain could register what has happened. This is a natural and healthy reflex. However, if you've had repeated painful experiences with a certain stimulus, your body may develop the muscle memory needed to protect you from suffering more pain, reflected as irrational fears, which can lead to irrational, self-sabotaging actions.

Now go back to your mental frameworks and think about what would happen if one of your mental frameworks considers rejection to be painful and therefore believes it must be avoided at all costs. Chances are you may develop conditional reflexes to protect yourself from rejections. Therefore, when you try to talk to someone you're attracted to or are about to knock on a door to make a sales call, your subconscious mind will set up a response to avoid potential rejections and bypasses your conscious brain. As a result, automatic impulses act on your body directly and release hormones into your bloodstream, putting you instantly in the "fight or flight" state of mind we talked about in the Brain Fuel section. The most unsettling thing here is that your conscious mind is forced to process these fearful and anxious emotions by rationalizing them, as what we found out during our exploration with the Split-Brain experiments of Michael Gazzaniga. Over time, these rationalizations crystalize into negative mental frameworks that keep us stuck in self-perpetuating cycles of subconscious self-sabotage.

Fortunately, you can train yourself to develop reflexes the same way an athlete or a performance artist masters a certain movement. Your positive frameworks create positive reflexes, and your brain starts filtering your experience based on these new frameworks. You start to see the world in a different light and your actions change. Before you realize it, your whole life starts to improve. What's even better is these changes don't require excessive willpower. Instead, they will become completely natural for you to integrate your thinking and your actions with your goals and your values as you build up your new reflexes. Your body becomes a participant in your thought process.

Recall the following progression covered in the Brain Fuel section:

1. Frameworks shape your filters.
2. Filters shape your perceptions.
3. Perceptions shape your thoughts.
4. Thoughts shape your actions.
5. Actions shape your habits.
6. Habits shape your life and your legacy.

Conditioned reflexes determine how your *subconscious mind* filters your experience and shapes your perception, thoughts, actions, habits, and eventually your life without your conscious mind ever realizing its influence. This is how brain intelligence becomes a part of your bodily intelligence. It's also why you can't change your behaviors and your life simply by changing your mindset. Instead, you must change how you fuel these subconscious reflexes and that's why Body Fuel is so important.

Below are three common examples of subconscious filtering:

- **Deletion.** Deletion happens when information that conflicts with your mental framework gets filtered out of your perception. As a result, you may not be able to recognize the amazing opportunities entering your life sometimes until it's too late. For the same reason, some people seem to only see what they "want" to see.

- **Distortion.** Distortion happens when your brain reinterprets information, so it fits your mental framework. For instance, if you're a man previously hurt by women, you might process a woman's kindness as a subtle form of manipulation. This, of course, is a distortion of reality. But to your mind, it can be more than legitimate.
- **Generalization**. Generalization means your brain is creating mental shortcuts to avoid thinking about difficult things in finer detail or to avoid potentially painful outcomes. If a dog bit you when you were ten, your brain might try to protect you by generalizing ***all*** dogs as dangerous.

All these filters are examples of how your subconscious mind alters your perception of reality, so it aligns with your deepest mental frameworks. Think back to the negative mental frameworks in the Brain Fuel section. Can you see how some might make you delete, distort, or generalize information, and therefore cause you to see the world differently than it is? Do you remember that your conscious mind can only process so much information at a time whereas your subconscious mind processes the rest of it? Furthermore, your subconscious mind, including the nerve impulses happening in your body, also initiate a physiological response in your nervous system that generates additional nerve signals that change how you feel about the world.

To make my point stronger, here's a mind-blowing example of how your subconscious mind changes your world view. Search for the video "Dove Real Beauty Sketches | You're more beautiful than you think[xviii]" on YouTube. In this video, a professional sketch artist listens to women describing their faces and sketches them according to their descriptions. He never sees their real faces, so all the sketches are based on how these women perceive themselves instead of their actual look. In nearly all cases, the sketch is much less beautiful. Why? Because our self-image stems from our mental frameworks and the filters generated by them. We don't see ourselves as we are. We see ourselves as we believe ourselves to be. The same applies to how we see the rest of the world. Therefore, confidence, the first of your Five Prime Capabilities can't be faked, nor can the Prime Capabilities of adaptability, resilience, focus, and leadership. They all must be developed.

Are you starting to see why it's so hard to change bad habits using only mental hacks? Because the more years we spend thinking a certain way, the more our brain ***and*** body become conditioned to those thoughts. Therefore, it takes more conscious power to change that way of thinking. However, it ***is*** possible to make changes once you start treating your entire body as one thinking organism instead of a machine that's simply commanded by your brain.

Think of your nervous system as a giant brain with cells that extends throughout your entire body. Like the Internet of Things, your body is a complex collection of specialized cells which transmit *and* receive information in nerve signals to and from other body parts *and* your brain.

Essentially, your body is an information network formed with cells. Your nervous system controls your body's organs, and your psychological and physical functions. It consists of two main parts: Central Nervous System (CNS) and Peripheral Nervous System (PNS). The CNS contains the brain and spinal cord while the PNS is comprised of the nerve fibers that connect the CNS to every other part of your body.

One division of your peripheral nervous system is your sympathetic nervous system. It controls your fight or flight responses that are usually linked to the conditioned reflexes. This is how irrational fears become automatic behaviors. When your brain initiates a reflex, your amygdala sends a "warning" signal that fires up your hypothalamus, it goes down your sympathetic nervous system and activates your adrenal glands. These glands then pump a messenger hormone called epinephrine (aka, adrenaline) into your bloodstream. These chemicals remain in your bloodstream for hours and affect your nervous system operation that influences your "thinking" in ways we discussed above. Few think about this fact when they consider what influence their thinking has on their actions ***and*** what conditioned reflexes they develop.

Additionally, your conditioned reflexes, along with all the thought impulses that travel between your body and brain, can affect the release of neurotransmitters, a messenger molecule that controls the impulses for eating, thinking, and certain ways of behaving. Therefore, trying to control these impulses with your conscious mind alone is like moving a cruise ship with a canoe paddle. To control your entire thinking organism, you must change the way you fuel your entire body including your gut-brain and peripheral nervous system. If you don't take conscious charge of your fueling, your base instincts will take over your life.

Think about the seemingly uncontrollable sugar craving we talked about earlier and how we seem to be incapable of overcoming that desire with only conscious willpower. **The average American consumes five times the daily sugar intake they should be having** (Natasa Janicic-Kahric of Georgetown University Hospital). Sugar over-consumption can impair brain function, memory, and learning skills. It can also lead to obesity, diabetes, and neurological diseases like Alzheimer's and dementia. Some researchers also found sugar to increase the risk of depression by causing a serotonin influx and disrupting your brain's chemical balance. So why can't we control our sugar consumption since most of us know that sugar is bad for us…? Because of the subconscious "thinking" processes we've talked about over the past few pages.

Thus, taking care of your brain and body with healthy habits and an optimized nervous system makes you more confident, adaptable, resilient, and focused. Healthy habits also enhance your memory, focus, clarity, creativity, and decision-making abilities, making you a more consistent and effective leader. For example, physical exercise can improve your brain's plasticity by promoting more nutrient flow through your astrocytes, the cells which nourish your neurons. A study conducted at the University of Adelaide in Australia[xix] enrolled a small group of people in their 20s and 30s in a 30-minute workout and found significant increase in their brains' neuroplasticity. That's because when we increase our heart rate during a workout, chemicals are released into the brain to create a euphoric feeling. This is an example of how body conditioning can create an extremely positive impact on your mental state and behaviors.

We can also reduce stress and anxiety by reducing the amount of cortisol, another messenger molecule released during stress and pumped into our brain. There are several ways to reduce cortisol and keep you from experiencing prolonged fight or flight episodes. These include the quality and regulation of your sleep, relaxation, recreational activities, healthy relationships, positive self-image frameworks, visualization, meditation, and more. This should tell you, once again, that your entire body is one intelligent organism, and you must fuel it properly for optimal health if you want to be physically ***and*** mentally healthy.

Meet Your "Thinking" Molecules

By now, you should know that thinking is more than something between your ears. Your body and brain operate as a single thinking organism and should be fueled as such. For example, hormones and neurotransmitters play a vital role in how your brain and your body process information and transfers that information between each other. Think of your neurotransmitters as billions of text messages being sent from one neuron in your body to another and eventually working their way through entire networks of neurons. Your neurons are equipped with tiny receptors for specific neurotransmitters, like tiny mailboxes that only receive a certain type of letter. Once a neurotransmitter has carried its message from one neuron to another, it is either reabsorbed into the sending neuron, or broken down by enzymes.

Certain chemicals can disrupt, enhance, or inhibit this process by blocking certain neuroreceptors, preventing reabsorption, or imitating your body's neurotransmitters. This results in an interruption in neurotransmitter transmission from one neuron to another. In other words, certain chemicals can disrupt your thinking processes. These chemicals are sometimes found in drugs whereas other times in food as well. Therefore, you may introduce chemicals into your system that fool your body and brain through your eating habits alone. These chemicals work in the same way “clickbait” stories on the internet fool people into arguing with each other over ridiculous things that aren’t true. As a result, to get this information process working in your favor, you must start treating your body like a thinking organism. You must remember that it will go to war with itself when fueled with the wrong information processing chemicals and sensory stimuli.

The Chemicals that Determines Your Thoughts and Behaviors

Are you starting to see how different this is than thinking of your body as a fuel burning machine that’s “driven” by your brain? Are you starting to see why it’s smart to frame thinking as something that happens throughout your brain *and* your body? I hope so, because it’s time to explore the primary neurotransmitter and hormones that influence the way you think, feel, and act.

Primary Neurotransmitters Influencing You

Dopamine is your reward chemical. It is critical to memory, learning, behavior, movement, and coordination. It tells your brain when you've achieved something significant. However, this chemical can also be released in response to negative behaviors like excessive sugar or alcohol consumption, thus tricking your brain into believing something bad is good for you.

Endorphins are your natural pain relievers. They inhibit pain signals and create the energized, euphoric feelings you experience after a good workout. Therefore, aerobic exercises are a great way to boost your endorphins. Regular aerobic exercise will put you into a longer and more frequent feel-good state and help reduce your stress.

Epinephrine is also known as adrenaline. It is one of your fight or flight chemicals that operates as a hormone or a neurotransmitter with a quick, lasting impact on your physiological state and your ways of thinking. Your body releases epinephrine in response to fear or stress, which leads to an increased heart rate, breathing, and blood flow in your brain and head. Thus, your face sometimes gets hot during high stress situations.

Norepinephrine is another fight or flight chemical and is very similar to epinephrine. The difference is that norepinephrine increases heart rate and the amount of blood pumped from the heart, which elevates your blood pressure, and helps you to break down fat and increase blood sugar levels, so you can deliver more energy to your muscles.

Glutamate is another excitatory neurotransmitter that

reinforces the synaptic connections between neurons. When this neurotransmitter is well-balanced, you're mentally sharper and often feel more confident.

Acetylcholine is another excitatory chemical that triggers muscle contractions, stimulates some hormones, and controls your heartbeat. It also plays a key role in brain function and memory. As an excitatory neurotransmitter, it uses choline as its building block.

GABA is a mood-regulating neurotransmitter with an inhibitory action that stops neurons from overexcitement. Low levels of GABA can cause anxiety, irritability, and restlessness.

Serotonin is another inhibitory chemical that regulates mood, appetite, blood clotting, sleeping, and your body's circadian rhythm. Since serotonin plays a role in depression and anxiety, Selective Serotonin Reuptake Inhibitors (SSRIs) can relieve depression by increasing serotonin levels in your brain. You can also naturally raise your serotonin level by exposing yourself to more sunlight and exercising regularly.

While these chemicals are necessary, excessive, or prolonged "doses" can create serious side-effects including depression, Alzheimer's disease, Parkinson's disease, heart diseases, and diabetes. Thankfully, you can control and balance your neurotransmitter response centers and create a more stable and fulfilling life with an appropriate diet, quality sleep, and exercise. If you can manage stress using the mental state practices from the last chapter on top of managing your neurotransmitter levels, you're well on your way to a happier brain and body.

Primary Hormones Affecting Your Life

Neurotransmitters aren't the only chemical messengers in your body. Your body is home to a much more complex chemical processing system with a mind-boggling effect on your physical and mental states, your immune system, your gut health, and all the other things we talked about. That system is called the endocrine system and it works through hormone production and transfer.

So, what are hormones? Hormones operate similarly as neurotransmitters, but with two major exceptions.

First, hormones are created and released by glands located in different places in your body. They are the "thinking" organs and critical functioning components in your endocrine system.

There are six major glands/organs that supports the "thinking" of your body.

The first organ is the pineal gland that secretes melatonin in the darkness, telling your body to relax and prepare for sleep. The melatonin production process can influence your circadian rhythms over time. However, if you sit up and stare at a computer (or smartphone screen) while in bed at night, your body releases cortisol (the stress hormone) instead of melatonin and keeps you awake and alert. Therefore, using electronic devices right before sleep will disrupt your sleep cycles, causing potential symptoms such as early onset insomnia.

Hypothalamus in your brain operates as the gateway between your brain and body. It has a front part, the anterior, and a back part, the posterior. It gives off many feel-good chemicals, including **endorphins and oxytocin**, which are also known as the love hormone that promotes good gut microbes growth and stimulates organs that secrete human growth hormones and promote cell growth. Another vital hormone your hypothalamus produces is the **antidiuretic hormone (ADH)**. ADH holds fluids inside your body. Once released, it travels to your kidneys and controls fluid excretion, getting toxins out of your body while keeping you hydrated.

Your thyroid gland gives off **T3 and T4 hormones that** accelerate your metabolism. In other words, that slow metabolism people talk about is more than genetics. It's also about how efficiently your thyroid is releasing these chemical messengers into your body. The thyroid also releases **calcitonin,** which is important for your metabolic feedback loops, making sure all your thinking centers are properly communicating with one another. Calcitonin also regulates the calcium levels in your bloodstream because bad blood calcium levels can be fatal. To put the thyroid's critical role into perspective, consider your endocrine system an orchestra and your thyroid the conductor. When your thyroid isn't working properly, it affects everything from your metabolism to muscle control, to nerve function, to bone health. Therefore, your thyroid is a key player in how gracefully you age. Many people ruin their thyroids with crash diets and other extreme weight loss or gaining systems. I'll soon reveal a simple way to make sure you don't fall into this trap.

Next is your pancreas which secretes insulin and glucagon hormones. These twin messenger hormones can lower or raise your blood sugar levels. This is vital for your energy level and your ability to control cravings to maintain a healthy weight. Remember, your cells have receptors for certain hormones and neurotransmitters. When you eat too much sugar, your body releases extra insulin to carry all that energy to your muscles. As a result, you develop insulin resistance where your insulin receptors will not absorb insulin as efficiently. When this happens, your body makes you believe that your blood sugar levels are lower than they really are, thus creating more cravings for sweet foods.

Your adrenal glands release glucocorticoids, which function as an anti-inflammatory agent. If you remember what we said about inflammation earlier, you'll understand why these are so important. Your adrenal glands also work in conjunction with your reproductive glands to release testosterone and estrogen, which have a dramatic influence on your metabolism. **It also releases two types of adrenalines: epinephrine and norepinephrine.** Most people have no idea that these are also considered neurotransmitters. In other words, your adrenal glands on top of your kidneys release a messenger molecule that influences the signals traveling through your nervous system, whereas we normally think this to be our brain's job only. Thus, this is another example of how your organs can influence your thinking, involuntary functions, and muscle memory development.

The last important organ in this group is your reproductive glands (testicles or ovaries), which release both testosterone and estrogen along with your adrenal glands. Testicles only release **testosterone**, while ovaries release both **testosterone and estrogen**. Why is this important? Because both estrogen and testosterone play an important role in your endocrine system, your physical health, and your mental health. Testosterone promotes lean muscle growth, bone mass, sex drive, and red blood cell production. Insufficient testosterone impacts your sexual performance, also your energy level and your ability to maintain lean muscles, which are critical in anti-aging as they are active tissues that burn fat and supports your limbs, thus preventing excessive stress on your joints. Likewise, low estrogen in men can lead to fatigue, anxiety, forgetfulness, irritability, and affects water retention. In women, low estrogen causes mood swings, hot flashes, depression, and other problems.

Second, when hormones enter your system, they have a significantly more lasting impact on your physiological state and thus, on how your body processes information. In other words, it controls your "metabolism." Some talk about metabolisms as if they are either "fast" or "slow" without knowing this is another false mental framework viewing your body as a fuel-burning machine, when your endocrine system operates more like a complicated computer network where data transmits from one unit to another, commanding specific functions in your body. Disruptions in this information network leads to many problems, both physically and mentally. Your brain and body form an indivisible system together. The thinking your body does influences what your brain does and vice versa. Therefore, fueling your capabilities and changing your life is more than mastering your mental processes. This ought to be a relief if you've struggled to make lasting changes using mental techniques alone.

Now, think about everything we just covered: inflammation, the gut-brain, and this new view of your subconscious mind. How do you think these might impact your mental states ***and*** your ability to perform at maximum potential when under pressure? Then think about the first promise I made to you in this book. I said you were going to have more of your best days more often. Now go back to what you just read on your ability to activate and maintain your "Flow State" at will. Are you starting to see why it's vital to fuel your brain ***and*** body like a single thinking organism?

I hope so. Because now that you're armed with clarity about how your body works, the habits for properly fueling your thinking organism are quite simple.

Winning the War Against Aging and Fatigue

Physical resilience makes all your Prime Capabilities easier to master. The secret to becoming physically resilient is to manage stress and keep inflammation under control. Remember the adrenal glands? They also serve as the anti-inflammatory producers. Too much time in "fight or flight" mode makes it harder for your body to keep inflammation down. Additionally, many of your conditioned reflexes are developed when your body processes ordinary or positive experiences as threats. Therefore, poor sleep and an unbalanced diet (especially the diet) are the most impactful on how your body produces inflammation.

For instance, gout, a form of reactionary arthritis, flares up when excessive uric acid crystallizes and deposits itself in the joints. It can be so painful and severe that you'd become unable to walk without crutches. It can also inflict lasting damage to your joints. While reactionary arthritis is rare in young people, it becomes much more common once you pass forty. Uric acid enters your bloodstream via foods like red meat and seafood. Under normal circumstances, your body digests these foods and passes the uric acid through sweat and urine. But if the messenger molecules are out of balance, or if you've spent too much time in "fight or flight" mode, your digestive system doesn't work as well. As a result, uric acid builds up.

But there's more to that.

When you don't eat enough vegetables, consume excessive processed foods and meats, and, on top of all, don't manage stress, your body becomes acidic and makes you more vulnerable to life-threatening diseases like cancer. Being highly acidic also makes you vulnerable to chronic inflammation, which, as we've already talked about, can cause serious problems with your physical ***and*** mental health. Even if you're not worried about this now, you'd be shocked to learn how much more susceptible you become as you age and as your endocrine system starts changing rapidly, while lean muscles loss accelerates.

Thus, the time to act is now. The good news is that managing inflammation and living a longer, more active life can be achieved with these 6 practices:

- **Healthy eating:** eating real food and accomplishing a healthy gut
- **Regular exercise:** strength and cardiovascular trainings 4-5 times a week
- **Stress management:** daily visualization and meditation practice
- **Regular sleep:** 8 hours a night + regular bed and waking times
- **Positivity:** having a positive mindset about your future
- **Fasting:** implementing your optimal fasting routine

I know that none of these are easy to control. But I never said fueling your body for good health was going to be easy to begin with. I said it was ***simple***. To reach your final goal, you must follow a certain order when approaching these habits, starting with your eating habits. Then, you add exercise, stress management, and regular sleep as you get your diet in order. Of course, you can try to do it all at once. But keep in mind that good health starts in your gut, thus it's best to start with your diet. If you aren't eating healthy foods, it will be hard to exercise consistently. You will also find it harder to recover from an intensive workout session. Likewise, if you try to manage stress without getting your eating and exercise habits in order first, you'll have a rather challenging time dealing with stress. With this, maintaining positivity about your future will help create a healthier physiological state, compared to one that is battling daily anxiety and nerves. Fasting has also joined this list in the recent years, as scientists are beginning to learn more about all the benefits, including anti-aging, of proper fasting practices. Finally, if you're not eating healthy and managing anxiety, your hormone levels and physiological state will make it harder for you to sleep ***and*** to wake up regularly. While this is going to take work, it could make all the difference in how well you live and when and how you die. Sleep is our time to recover and recharge.

Remember, inflammation depletes energy and makes you prone to mental health problems. Therefore, it becomes harder to remain confident and focused. Inflammation can also dramatically impact how gracefully you age and how vulnerable you are to physical and mental illnesses, some of which are life-threatening. Chronic inflammation also makes it nearly impossible to exit the Survival Mindset and enter the Growth Mindset. There are also other benefits of regular sleep, exercise, stress management, and good nutrition. For example, they promote a healthy and well-balanced gut microbiome, optimizing your "gut-brain," and give you more control over your dietary choices, your conditioned reflexes, and your conscious mental capabilities.

Remember, your conscious mind is no match for your subconscious mind. You need both working in harmony and that starts with adopting the mental framework that treats your entire body as an intelligent extension of your mind. Once you start aligning your habits with these frameworks, your personal growth accelerates, and you become immune to self-sabotage.

That said, let's look at some practical actions for fueling your brain and body, and mastering all your Prime Capabilities.

Body Fuel and Your Five Prime Capabilities

We've already talked about how your gut-brain influences your willpower and your general sense of happiness. Nothing impacts your gut-brain more than your diet. Your body also rebuilds its tissues using materials from the food you eat—so this relates to how resilient you can be.

When it comes to diet, there are two things you absolutely must know and remember.

#1: Everyone is Different

We have different genes. Therefore, there is not one specific diet everyone should be on. Professional athletes, models, and celebrities almost always have personal trainers, nutrition coaches, and endocrinologists helping them customize their meal plans. This is not a coincidence. Therefore, as an ordinary person who doesn't have these resources, you must do additional research about your body type and perhaps talk to a holistic doctor about your specific situation, or at least find someone with the knowledge and expertise on tailoring individual dietary goals according to body types.

For instance, you should have your gut health, hormones, and your muscular and cardiovascular health assessed periodically by a professional. It is true that online surveys and self-diagnosis questionnaires are easier and cheaper. But they are not at all comparable to working with someone experienced in assessing all the nuances of your health. In the next few pages, I will share with you some of the most valuable universal recommendations I learned from nutritionists and doctors that will help you take the first steps toward unleashing your most abundant mind and biological capabilities.

Remember, your gut consists of bacteria that act as dictators of what you eat, how you absorb, and how you digest. These bacteria formulate over time based on individual diets. A poor diet leads to the growth of bad gut bacteria who send signals to your brain, so you crave more of the same unhealthy food and drink. What we eat also determines how the bacteria harvest nutrition and chemicals. This gives an entirely new dimension to the saying "you are what you eat." Your current biological makeup is partially controlled by your genetics, but also by your cumulative eating decisions. Everyone has different genetic dietary histories. So, it's important to say no to one-size-fits-all diet advice. Although there is one universal truth when it comes to our eating habits.

#2: Real Food vs Fake Food

"You are What You Eat."

One of the most destructive mental frameworks in the western culture is that anything found in the food section of the grocery store is considered food by default, when in fact some "foods" are merely well-packaged and well-marketed chemicals made to taste good. Eating healthy starts with dumping this dogma and setting a higher standard about what is food and what isn't.

There are only two types of food. First, there's food that grows out of the ground. If you can grow something on a farm, pick it off a tree, a bush, or out of the ground, that's the first type of real food. Second, there's food that *eats* the first type of food, such as animals living on the earth or in the water and eat plants or other animals.

Chips, candy, soda, crackers, candy bars, fry batter, and dozens of other "foods" don't fit into either category. Rather, they're masterpieces of chemical engineering, designed for a long shelf life with an addictive taste. The same goes for many meat products. For example, cows are supposed to eat grass. Their digestive systems aren't naturally made to process foods like corn and grains, and they're certainly not meant to be stuck with needles, pumped with hormones. Yet this is exactly what many meat manufacturers do to their animals. The discussion of humane treatment aside, since many animals are not eating real food, the meat they produce can't be considered real either.

When you eat something produced or removed from an animal, you are essentially eating the cumulative result of everything the animals consumed. Your body can have a variety of reactions to these hormones and chemicals, and most of them are not good for you. In other words, you don't just eat what you eat, you also eat what *it* ate.

Therefore, if you want to improve your gut health, try adopting this "eat real food" mental framework. Make it the foundation of your shopping and eating routines.

"You are what you eat, ate."

Dishonest Foods

Remember, barely any additives and chemicals in processed foods are there to make you healthier. Their purpose is to give the food a longer shelf-life and make it more addictive. There's even an occupation called "Food Chemistry[xx]," which is the study of how biological and non-biological components in fake and real foods interact with one's body. Food companies spend a lot of money hiring these experts to figure out how to make their food more addictive to the human mind and body. For example, your gut produces 90% of serotonin, your "happy" chemical. Have you ever wondered why certain tasty but bad foods make you feel happy? Do you think the people who sell these foods haven't thought of this? Of course, they have! It's their business. The very experience of eating fake food can become addictive, too. Sugar spikes your dopamine and serotonin levels, which is why people keep going back to sweets for comfort. Once that sugar high wears off, you experience a withdrawal from those positive chemicals and the cravings rise again. So, you eat again and on it goes until sugar consumption becomes a reflex. The same goes with trans fats and other processed chemicals.

On top of this, food companies aren't *necessarily* obligated by law to disclose what's in their foods. High-fructose corn syrup (HFCS), for instance, is one of the worst "false foods" out there. Yet food companies call it by several different names on food labels and are not obligated to reveal ON the label if the HFCS amount is below a certain level, even though when you eat enough "foods", the amount you consume can easily go far above a safe level. How many "undercover" names are there for HFCS alone? It's impossible to trace because the manufacturers are constantly coming up with new ways to trick us. But here are a few alternative names[xxi] used in the past for your reference:

- Isoglucose.
- Natural corn syrup.
- Maize syrup.
- Fructose syrup.
- Fructose isolate.
- Fructose.
- Glucose syrup.
- Fruit fructose.
- Crystalline fructose.

It's futile to try to list all the ingredients you should look out for when reading food labels because it would require a much longer book plus personal research at times to understand food labeling. Therefore, as you think about your diet and what is most beneficial, limiting the number of foods you eat can have a strong impact on your body's performance and make it easier when shopping for groceries. Your body and stomach bacteria get into a routine of processing the foods you're used to eating. On the other hand, eating real foods can reduce inflammation and improve insulin sensitivity, improving your health and decreasing your cravings. Foods such as dairy, grains, corn, soy, artificial flavors, and sugars are known to create mild to high levels of inflammation. As we discussed briefly in the last chapter, these unhealthy habits of causing inflammation from food can have serious implications for your health.

How to Get on a Healthier Diet

When I changed my diet a few years ago, the change of my health was one of the biggest factors I experienced. After playing relatively intensive basketball in my 30s, I was always very sore after playing several games, and my body would ache the next day. But as I changed my diet, I was amazed at how quickly my body was healing and recovering. I no longer felt the typical intense soreness and aches the day after unless I was physically banged up. In addition to eating real foods, here is a list of things you can do to get your inflammation and cravings under control.

1. **Get your gut microbes tested.** Don't tell yourself it's "too expensive to do that right now." Just do it. Medical bills are one of the leading causes of personal bankruptcy later in life, so if you think you can't afford it now, there is no way you would be able to afford bigger, more expensive health problems as you age.

2. **Create a cleansing strategy.** Your body is likc your house. If you don't clean it regularly, you may get sick from the dust, dirt, and pollution. That said, you will need an ongoing practice for cleansing your body. Daily doses of apple cider vinegar, lemon juice, trace minerals (drinkable forms are best), fish oils, and periods of intermittent fasting are all highly effective cleansing strategies.

3. **Eat real food.** Next time you go grocery shopping, ask yourself how you'd acquire that same food if you were living off the land as a hunter or gatherer. If you could have picked it from a plant, grown it in a garden, or hunted it down with a spear or bow and arrow, buy it. Think twice before bringing anything else home no matter how tempting it appears to be.

4. **Switch to water and organic tea.** Most food advertising is spent marketing sugary drinks because they benefit the manufacturers, not consumers. Sodas aside, most juices can be almost as bad since you're absorbing larger than natural amounts of sugar at once. Therefore, try to drink mostly water at the ratio of one ounce per pound or two of body weight. On average, 80-140 ounces per day.

5. **Take probiotics and prebiotics**. Probiotics will give you beneficial bacteria that align your digestive tract and support your body's ability to absorb nutrients and fight infections. Good microbes also make you crave good food and thus promote a healthier brain and endocrine system. Prebiotics fuel your healthy bacteria with fiber from certain foods.

6. **Add *natural* supplements to your diet**. While I agree that some supplements are great, you simply can't supplement your way out of a bad diet. However, once you've built up some momentum with your eating habits by adopting the first five methods, you may add some natural supplements to boost and maintain the effect.

(Which I'll provide a short list in the coming pages)

Stay Alert, Stay Healthy

Another thing you'd want to do is keep a list of fake food and a list of healthy food. Take both lists with you when you eat out or go shopping.

Your "no go" list might include:

Ingredient	Sources
Refined sugar and sweeteners	low fat yogurt, BBQ sauce, fruit juices,granola
High-fructose corn syrup (HFCS)	Ketchup, teriyaki sauce, cereal, candy, frozen meals, soda, and many other products.
Highly processed oils	
Gluten	pastas, noodles, breads, pastries, crackers,cereal
Artificial trans-fat	Vegetable shortening, margarines and vegetable oils, fried fast foods, non-dairycreamers
Low fiber foods,refined foods	refined white flour/bread, white pasta, white sugar
High glycemic	white bread, rice cakes, crackers, and mostpackaged cereals
Harmful chemicals	glyphosate, polysorbate 80, lecithin, carrageenan, polyglycerols, and xanthan

To build your own list, I recommend you conduct some research based on your current eating habits. The more extensive and thorough the list, the easier it is for you to avoid bad food.

Likewise, start building a list of good foods to work into your diet. Try some healthy food that you don't like and get acquainted with their taste. Remember, your microbes control your food cravings. For example, if you hate spinach, it's probably because your gut is populated with microbes that love sweet, greasy, fatty foods instead of vegetables. But as you start replacing these bad microbes with good ones, your interest in healthy food will improve. Even if your cravings don't change, it's still smart to eat for your health instead of to superficial satisfaction. For instance, eating broccoli has almost no immediate emotional reward. But broccoli is rich in compound glucosinolates, which the body breaks down to produce isothiocyanates that help prevent neurodegenerative diseases. Therefore, don't eat to satisfy your taste buds. Instead, eat with the goal of fueling your gut-brain. Your body will eventually catch up and you'll start to enjoy healthy food.

A few examples of healthy foods include:

Item	**Details**
Phytochemicals	plants, can protect cells from damage andeven heart disease and cancer
Brain-boosting food	fatty cold-water fish, foods with omega 3 fats
Berries	Especially blueberries
Cruciferous vegetables	broccoli, spinach, kale, and other leafyvegetables
seeds and most nuts	almonds, walnuts, brazil nuts, hazelnuts
Green tea	

You should also add some inflammation-fighting and endocrine-optimizing spices to this list, such as cinnamon, turmeric, ginger, cayenne pepper, ginkgo, vinpocetine, etc. Again, this list is just an example. You should build your own list according to your body conditions.

Your diet affects your thinking and your energy, focus, and willpower. Multiple studies have found a correlation between a high-refined-sugar-diet and impaired brain function, which can likely lead to mood disorders, depression, and other mental health issues.

However, studies also suggest the quality of the foods consumed over one's lifetime affects your brain's structure and functions. For instance, consuming omega-3 fatty acids found in fish supports neuron maintenance. They are also essential for the information transmission between brain cells. In contrast, food rich in sugar and saturated fat can promote oxidative stress, which damages cell membranes. Also, cells use glucose, amino acids (the building blocks of protein), and fat for energy. Without glucose, your brain wouldn't be able to work well. After your body has used the energy it needs, the leftover glucose is stored in little bundles called glycogen in the liver and muscles. Your body can store enough fuel for about a day. Therefore, eating healthy can help you stay sharp and focused, manage your weight, and explode your performance and your momentum[xxii].

Finally, start your day by drinking 12-24 ounces of lemon water. It prepares your digestive system for the incoming food throughout your day. Staying hydrated also protects your joints and soft tissues from injury, especially during workouts. Water also delivers nutrients that aid in cartilage and other soft tissue repair whereas dehydration wears and tears your cartilage that supports joints like your knees. Over time, new cell generation fails to catch up and often leads to soft tissue injuries[xxiii] like meniscus tears. Dehydration can also weaken your immune system. On average, your body needs two liters of water every day. Your body is mostly made of water. The same goes for your brain, which is approximately 80% water. Therefore, a well-hydrated body operates more efficiently and is less prone to injury and disease.

Of course, once you get your diet in order, you can add natural supplements. So, let's finish this section with some supplements that will boost your energy level:

Ashwagandha	Rhodiola Rosea	Coenzyme Q10
Vitamin B12, B6and Niacin	Calcium and Vitamin D3	Magnesium
Iron	Citrulline	Beetroot powder
Melatonin	Tyrosine	Caffeine with L-Theanine
Lion's Mane mushrooms	Green Tea extract	Oils from coconut,avocado and olives

Just remember that you can't out-supplement a bad diet. Your body is a thinking *organism,* and you want it working in harmony with your brain. So, let food be your FIRST source of medicine and your primary energy source. Fuel yourself with a healthy diet by eating real food and avoiding fake ones. These two habits alone will solve most of the problems that make you prone to injury, aging, and disease. And if you don't have the mental resolve to eat healthy all the time, don't worry. It ***will*** get easier as your brain and body start to "think" in a way that serves your goal to be healthy. It's up to you to get your body working with you.

Regular Exercises: Fueling Your Body for Youth and Longevity

Have you ever thought about how your body ages? It's closest to a loss or degradation of information. For example, a photocopy of a document never looks as good as the original.

If you make a copy of that copy, you'd lose more quality. This degradation worsens every time you make a copy of the previous copy until you end up with a document that looks nothing like the original. We age in a similar way. Your body doesn't "wear down" the way an industrial machine does, but instead loses the quality of your biological information.

For instance, studies[xxiv] in 2013 found that the malfunction of a proteins family, sirtuins is a central cause of aging. Sirtuins are responsible for DNA repair and cellular health management by keeping cells on task. Overworked cells cause symptoms of aging, such as organ failure and wrinkles. As our body gets older, it loses the ability to interpret genetic information and our cells begin to run low on Nicotinamide Adenine Dinucleotide (NAD). NAD is a dinucleotide found in all cells that is essential to your metabolism. NAD also activates sirtuins. Modern research tells us that by the time you reach 60, your NAD levels are about half of what they used to be during your 40s. We've been talking about the body as an intelligent information processing system. Therefore, aging is ultimately a degradation of information processing quality.

Thankfully, you can slow down this degradation and even recover some of the lost information simply by changing your diet and daily activities. Healthy stressors, such as exercises, can increase NAD levels and promote sirtuin activity. Thus, you often hear how exercise prolongs life expectancy. But that's not all. Lean muscle also consumes energy even while you're resting, making it harder for your body to store that energy as fat. This also explains why people gain more weight as they get older. It's not so much that they're gaining weight, but more because they're losing lean muscles. Also, exercise is a general necessity for a healthy life. It delivers oxygen and nutrients to your tissues and makes your cardiovascular system more efficient. It also helps keep your thinking, learning, and judgment skills sharp even as you age. As you achieve more success, you will face many critical decisions on a weekly even daily basis. Your ability to stay sharp and make good decisions is vital to living an abundant life, whereas bad choices will hold you back from all that you deserve to accomplish in this life. Without exercising, your cognitive ability decreases, affecting how you learn, remember, and make decisions. Exercise also triggers the BDNF (brain-derived neurotrophic). Here's a statement from the National Library of Medicine[xxv] about why this is important.

The BDNF gene provides instructions for making a protein found in the brain and spinal cord called brain-derived neurotrophic factor. This protein promotes the survival of nerve cells (neurons) by playing a role in the growth, maturation (differentiation), and maintenance of these cells. In the brain, the BDNF protein is active at the connections between nerve cells (synapses), where cell-to-cell communication occurs. The synapses can change and adapt over time in response to experience, a characteristic called synaptic plasticity. The BDNF protein helps regulate synaptic plasticity, which is important for learning and memory. The BDNF protein is found in regions of the brain that control eating, drinking, and body weight; the protein likely contributes to the management of these functions.

Our neural circuits act as the information highways between different areas of the brain. Neurons communicate with one another by sending chemicals, the neurotransmitters we discussed, through synapses, the junction between two nerve cells. How these neurons communicate with one another by making connections throughout the brain is what makes each of us unique in how we think, feel and act. Without delving too deep into the neuron makeup of biology, this is a quick summary of what's taking place on a cellular level in your brain. Depending on the habits you're administering (especially with food and exercise), will depend on the circuitry health of your neural network.

To increase the BDNF levels in your body and brain:

1. Manage your weight. Good eating habits
2. Rigorous exercise
3. Curcumin, Green tea, Omega 3s, Resveratrol (found in grapes, wine, dark chocolate, pistachios, blueberries, and peanuts
4. Sunlight
5. Quality social engagement

https://www.psychologytoday.com/us/blog/balanced/202001/the-link-between-bdnf-and-neuroplasticity

The importance of exercise can't go unnoticed and is a large part of every aspect of human health. It purifies your body. When you exercise, lymph fluids circulate through the body and removes toxins and other harmful materials. During exercises, you naturally absorb more oxygen and make room for that additional oxygen. In return, your cells kick out toxins that are taking up the space.

Most personal trainers and fitness experts break the practice of good exercise into three components:

- **Intensity:** how hard you exercise.
- **Duration:** how long you exercise.
- **Frequency:** how often you exercise.

We will break these down one by one so you can start taking practical actions today.

#1: Exercise Intensity

Exercise intensity begins with setting goals and working toward achieving them, while continuing to set new goals as you achieve the old ones to ensure that you're always pushing your body beyond its current limits. This system also keeps you from getting bored with the same routines.

For example, if you have 20 minutes to walk a mile, set a goal to speed-walk the same distance in 15 minutes. Once you accomplish that, try jogging one mile in 12 minutes. If you reach the point where you can no longer reduce your time, set a different type of goal like extending the distance or combining it with another exercise. The same structure applies no matter where you start.

Change your exercise routine to shock your muscles. The more you set, track, and achieve new goals, the more you see visual representations of your progress. This doesn't have to be an elaborate system of notes. But it should at the very least include some form of goal setting, progress tracking, and result evaluation.

Also, make sure your goals relate to performance. This way, it challenges you to exercise with more intensity. For example, it's fine to have a goal to lose thirty pounds, but this is not a performance goal. Instead, it's an outcome or a result. If you constantly set, track, and achieve new performance goals, losing that weight will be easier and more enjoyable. This also allows you to use your workout as a means of achieving specific health goals like losing weight. Having a specific result in mind will inspire you to enhance your intensity and push yourself harder.

Within this intensity realm, lies limitations and opportunities. There's a reason many peak performers push their bodies to perform marathons, ironmans, triathlons, crossfit competitions, mountain climbing and many others. Most of them are testing their body's limits and pushing them into optimal states that can extend physical and mental capacities. I'm not suggesting that everyone sign up for the next race, but to think about how you're challenging the intensity of your workouts to maximize health and the benefits that come with it.

#2: Exercise Duration

Your exercise duration depends on your body type and your current fitness level. While workout is positive for the most part, it's still a form of stress and thus also causes your body to release stress hormones such as cortisol. Therefore, if you work out for longer than sixty to ninety minutes per session, your body can release excessive cortisol which can impede your digestion, recovery, or the balance of your endocrine system. But as I said a moment ago, your exercise duration should depend mostly on your body type. Usually working out too long isn't an issue. 30-45 minutes at least 4 days a week is recommended.

#3: Exercise Frequency

The most suitable exercise frequency is different for everyone. Some people work out every other day (Monday, Wednesday, Friday, and Saturday), taking 3 days off a week. 4 to 5 days a week is also a great measure. Others work out 5-6 days a week but split their days up according to muscle groups. For example:

- **Day 1:** chest, biceps, triceps, and light cardio
- **Day 2:** back, abs, and stretching
- **Day 3:** heavy cardio workout
- **Day 4:** legs (quads, hams, calves), core and stretching
- **Day 5:** shoulders, biceps, triceps, and light cardio

Once again, you can adjust your fitness schedule according to your body type and fitness goals. Ultimately, finding your optimal exercise frequency is like finding your optimal diet — it depends on your body and your fitness level. Therefore, athletes might work out a lot more than ordinary people while having different goals. So, if you're not sure how often to exercise, ask your body. Get something that monitors your HRV (heart rate variability) and tells you when your body is sufficiently rested for another workout. This way, you're letting the incredibly complex "intelligence" within your body to tell you when to work out, rest and recover.

Body Types[xxvi]

Body Type #1: Ectomorph

Ectomorphs are long and lean. They have a faster metabolism and therefore burn more quickly and easily. However, ectomorph bodies have a tough time building and maintaining lean muscles. Therefore, ectomorphs might do best spending 30 to 45 minutes on strength training and 15 to 20 minutes on cardiovascular training each session.

Body Type #2: Endomorphs

Endomorphs are bulkier and often pear-shaped. They build raw power and muscles easier than ectomorphs but tend to accumulate and hold onto body fat. Therefore, endomorphs might do best spending 30 to 45 minutes on cardiovascular training, and 15 to 20 minutes on strength training.

Body Type #3: Mesomorphs

Mesomorphs are well-built with highly responsive muscle cells. They can build lean muscle and burn fat equally well. Other than being mere mortals, they really don't have any significant weaknesses when it comes to physical fitness. Therefore, Mesomorphs can split up their workout hour depending on whether their goal is to burn fat or build muscle.

Which body type are you? That's a question you'll want to discuss with a fitness expert. An expert will tell you that almost no one represents the perfect example of a single body type. Rather, most people are a cross between two types. So, it's important to consult someone who can help you assess your body type even if you don't work with them for ongoing training.

If you can't see an expert and aren't sure where to begin with your exercise duration, check out The American Heart Association's fitness recommendations[xxvii]. They suggest 150 minutes of moderate aerobic exercise and 75 minutes of vigorous aerobic activity per week.

Stress Management and Sleep

The more studies are conducted on sleep, the more obvious that sleep is a key factor for a healthy and abundant life. In fact, sleep deprivation is a common strategy used to make people more susceptible to new mental or emotional conditioning. It's used in the military, especially during war-time interrogations.

Now, remember that a healthy diet and a good exercise program are essential to both stress reduction and sleep enhancement. Exercise is a positive form of stress. The more you train your body to deal with physical stress, the better it will be in managing emotional stress. Meanwhile, the mental state and visualization practice we covered in the section on brain fuel are incredible strategies for training your mind and body to eliminate and manage stress.

Recent studies have surfaced in the past few years, detailing America's number one health problem, stress. In fact, up 75% - 90% of doctor visits are related to stress related issues. Managing stress effectively is then arguably the most significant element to focus on as you prepare to level up and achieve more. Anyone that seeks to push themselves out of their comfort zone to pursue desired goals, also needs a plan for managing the stress along the way. That's why having a holistic approach to your capability development journey is essential to level up effectively. If you don't, stress hormones can shut off your immune system (made up of your special organs, cells and chemicals), that fight infection and disease. The number one way to weaken your immune system is a lack of stress management.

In addition, your gut health plays a significant role as well in sleep. Experts who have been studying the microbiome are finding increasing evidence detailing the regulation of sleep and how it's directly correlated to the "gut-brain axis." Dr. Mayer of the book *The Mind-Gut Connection,* says that the gut's microorganisms seem to possess several signaling mechanisms that allow them to communicate with the brain in ways that influence a person's mood, appetite, stress levels, and much more. "One of our hypotheses is that these bacteria produce metabolites that go back to the brain," he says. Therefore, to reduce stress and sleep better, it is critical that you understand the power of gut health once again.

https://www.everydayhealth.com/sleep/how-do-the-bacteria-in-my-gut-affect-my-sleep/

Stress management and sleep go hand in hand and we'll talk about both in this section. We'll also cover other practices to further help you manage and reduce stress in the Spirit Fuel and Social Fuel sections later.

The Habit of Getting Regular Sleep

Similar to your diet and workouts, the minimum sleep required for each person differs as well. However, our basic need for proper levels of deep sleep and REM sleep doesn't change. Deep sleep and REM sleep are both critical to our body's ability to heal and perform. It's also important to sleep in healthy intervals rather than staying up for long periods of time, then making up for it by sleeping excessively. Simply put, you should pay attention to the three fundamental characteristics of your sleeping behavior:

- **Intensity:** how deeply you sleep.
- **Duration:** how long you sleep.
- **Frequency:** how often you sleep.

Most people think the secret to a good night's sleep is to manage their schedule. But how many times have you managed your schedule well, gone to sleep at a good hour, only to lie awake at night unable to fall asleep? How many times have you slept the entire night and still had a hard time getting up in the morning? More importantly, how many times have you been exhausted and sleep-deprived, but ***still*** had trouble getting sleep? Sleep isn't just about managing your schedule or any other external factors. It's about managing the *internal* processes that control your sleep and wake cycles.

Remember what we talked about earlier. Your pineal gland releases melatonin which helps you sleep. But it only releases melatonin in response to darkness. Likewise, your body wakes up by releasing excitatory chemicals like cortisol. Your body is also more likely to be alert and anxious if you're stuck in the fight or flight state. So, the question is: how can you manage your hormone levels and mental state so that your body finds it easier to fall asleep?

The simple answer lies behind the three characteristics. Let's look at them one by one.

#1: Sleep Intensity

The single most important criteria for maintaining and strengthening your memory function is quality, substance-free sleep. This deep sleep (REM) state is when you sleep, recover, and clear out waste from the mind. It also allows your brain to restore its chemical balance. A lack of quality sleep can negatively affect the hormones related to satiation even if you're sleeping the right number of hours. For example, when you don't get enough *quality* sleep, ghrelin, a hormone which increases appetite, goes up and leptin, a hormone that suppresses appetite, goes down. As a result, you crave more unhealthy, high calorie snacks and foods. This will further upset your endocrine system, creating a vicious negative cycle that makes it harder to get quality sleep.

To get quality sleep, you will first want to set aside uninterrupted sleeping time so you can reach the REM stage. Quality sleep isn't just about not feeling tired but being chemically balanced and recharged. For example, men's testosterone production is also dependent on getting three hours of uninterrupted sleep because the production slows down during the day. Therefore, men need quality sleep to restore healthy testosterone levels. Uninterrupted sleep also produces cytokines, a protective, infection-fighting substance associated with immune system health. Cytokines are used by your body to fight bacteria and viruses contracted. They are also known to provide additional energy to the immune system to boost its strength to fight illness. However, when not properly regulated, cytokines can lead to chronic inflammation. Therefore, quality sleep reduces undesired inflammation.

Second, the darker it is when you're sleeping, the better. That's because your pineal gland releases melatonin in response to darkness but excitatory hormones like cortisol in response to light. Therefore, you must try to get less exposure to light as you're falling asleep and during your sleeping stage. Meanwhile, it's vital to get daily exposure to natural sunlight, especially in the mornings and early afternoon so your body knows what time of day it is and can prepare itself for the regular cycle of waking and sleeping.

#2: Sleep Duration

For most of us, the average sleep duration needed is seven to eight hours a night. However, most people don't know why we're sometimes tired despite having gotten the proper amount of sleep. In his book *Sync*, author and scientist Steven Strogatz unpacks some shocking sleep studies that challenge the common mental frameworks about sleeping.

First, the studies revealed that our sleep patterns have little to do with how much we slept or how tired we feel. It's our core body temperature that decides our sleeping patterns. Also, there are times of the day that are more suitable for sleeping than others. For example, people are mentally slower between 3:00 to 5:00 a.m. Even if you overcome your urge to sleep and get a "second wind," your body still completes its natural circadian cycle, just without the sleep. When this happens, your alertness returns, your body rises, and cortisol is released the same way it would if you'd just woke up from a full night's sleep. So, science reveals that having a regular bedtime between 9 and 10 pm, and a waking time around 5:00 or 6:00 am is the best way to keep your body and brain in rhythm.

#3: Sleep Frequency

Your sleep frequency would most likely take care of itself if you can handle the intensity and duration parts by getting into a regular sleeping rhythm in sync with your natural circadian rhythm. But I do suggest you work on getting into a routine of going to bed at the same time and getting up at the same time. Also, try not to eat within the few hours before going to bed, especially food that requires a lot of digestion. Digestion is harder work for the body than most people realize. Therefore, if your body is digesting while you're sleeping, it has less energy to spend on the crucial functions we talked about earlier. In other words, be intentional about what you eat at night. High sugar or carbohydrate foods can cause an influx in your glucose running through your body and keeping you alert when you should be sleeping.

If you fall off the schedule, don't worry. You don't need to make up for lost sleep because your circadian rhythms respond to body temperature changes more than anything else. So, focus on getting your ***internal*** rhythms instead of your external schedule alone in sync. The more natural your sleeping rhythm becomes, the easier it will be to manage your schedule to support your new habits.

Intermittent Fasting[xxviii]: Fueling by Not Fueling

Fasting one meal a day several days a week can bring magical benefits for your long-term health.

Digestion and absorption of nutrients requires a lot of work from your body and consumes a lot of energy. If you give your body a break every now and then, your body will redirect that energy toward something miraculous: prolonging your life.

Yes, intermittent fasting is the "fuel" that can give you more time on earth and more energy to use to achieve your intentions.

Clinical studies have shown that eating less leads to a longer lifespan. While there are still conflicting theories as to *why* this happens, it's important to focus on what we ***do*** know. For example, we know that eating less and regular fasting allows your digestive organs to rest and gives your body more energy for fueling your brain, as well as building and maintaining lean muscle. When you fast, your body adjusts hormone levels for easier access to fat stored. Your growth hormone levels increase significantly from fasting and calorie reduction, helping you lose weight and produce muscles. Calorie reduction and intermittent fasting also increase insulin sensitivity and thus lower your insulin level significantly. Most critically, your cells go through a repair process during fasting, shedding old and defective proteins while making room for the regeneration of healthy cells, even increasing your sirtuin levels. Considering how much work your body does when it's digesting and absorbing food, these results are no surprise. The energy saved via fasting needs to go somewhere. Therefore, fasting is a great way to redirect your energy toward recovery and longevity.

Thankfully, intermittent fasting isn't some mysterious spiritual discipline. All you need to do is fast breakfast or dinner three or four times a week while setting aside one or two days a month for a full-day fast if you want to step up your intensity. Breakfast being the most common fasting practice, fasting for 13-17 hours, from dinner to lunch the next day. I know we all had it hammered into our heads that "breakfast is the most important meal of the day[xxix]." But how often do we think about where that saying came from? It will open your eyes if you look into food lobbyists' roles in getting that idea into the mainstream consciousness. Most of our knowledge on how to eat came to us from people who make money selling food. That's why when it comes to your health, it's smarter to let science speak louder than marketing. Try fasting one meal three or four times a week and see for yourself how much more energy you have than you would after a heavy meal. Do this a few times a week for 3-6 months and let your body tell you whether it's a good idea to keep up this habit. Just remember, any time you make a change like this, your body can create misinform you about what it really needs. Those cravings you have while your fasting is a great example. The more you condition your body this way, the more it will agree with the changes you're making.

Think about the word BREAKFAST. Break-your-Fast.

Changing our eating routines creates a neurochemical and hormonal change that can lead to cravings and uncomfortable feelings, but once your body adjusts to it, it becomes easier.

Change is never easy but this is one of my favorite adjustments I've incorporated into my human performance approach.

Your Prime Capabilities Revisited

At the beginning of this section, we talked about how your brain and body should operate as a single system, working in harmony to achieve your goals. It's also wiser to think of your body as an intelligent organism instead of a machine driven by your brain alone. Billions of nerve cells and messenger molecules are rushing information between the cells of your body as you read these words. This biological information tells your body and brain how to respond to your environment, fight infections, rebuild tissues, digest food, absorb nutrients, and perform dozens of other crucial functions. By now, you should realize that everything starts with changing your mental framework and fueling your body according to that new framework. Therefore, a better question to ask would be, is your body in the habit of thinking in a way that increases your Five Prime Capabilities.

1. **Confidence**
2. **Adaptability**
3. **Resilience**
4. **Focus**
5. **Leadership**

As we discussed, mental shortcuts or mind-over-matter techniques alone aren't enough. You must fuel and train your body so that it's subconscious thinking process works automatically, so you can maximize these capabilities and activate your Master Capability. This leads us to another equally important question. When answered, it will bring you a new level of clarity, courage, and insight that few people ever achieve in their lifetime. The question is:

How do you get your brain, body, and spirit aligned towards achieving your Primary Intention?

CHAPTER 6: SPIRIT FUEL

"What we commonly call man, the eating, drinking, planting, counting man, does not, as we know him, represent himself, but misrepresents himself. Him we do not respect, but the soul, whose organ he is, would he let it appear through his action, would make our knees bend."

— Ralph Waldo Emerson, *The Oversoul*

"Humanity follows earth; earth follows heaven; heaven follows Tao; Tao follows only itself."

— *Tao Te Ching*, Chapter 25

"Thy Kingdom come, thy will be done—on earth as it is in heaven."

— Jesus of Nazareth, John 17: 22-23

A chapter on spirituality might seem out of place in a book on human performance, but this chapter isn't about religion.

As someone who grew up a Christian, I understand the controversy religious association can create. One of my beliefs in life is that the influences we grow up with, including our religion, tend to stick with us into adulthood. If I would have grown up a Buddhist, the chances of me remaining Buddhist would be high. If I grew up in Hinduism, I'd probably still be practicing Hinduism. The same goes for most religions. Thankfully, almost everyone, including non-religious individuals, will agree that a discussion about spirituality regarding the following common threads is appropriate.

First, religious communities indeed provide support to the individual and even the society altogether. They also encourage accountability among organizations, individuals, and communities. Second, religious communities unite under a common set of values, which is essential for any healthy community to thrive. However, like any other institution where power and influence flows, a religion sometimes attracts people who are eager to gain power over others and over the society. Meanwhile, we will focus on using spirituality to gain power over only one person — yourself. If you make this your focus, you'll soon be able to influence and lead others through inspiration instead of coercion. Therefore, the definition of spirituality used in this section will be one that is consistent with the goal of this book.

"**Spirituality** is connecting to a greater power with the purpose of expressing that power through our actions."

It is up to you what this "higher power" is as long as you agree with the three fundamental rules of spirituality listed below.

First, no matter what higher power you believe in, it is either the source or the foundation of the material universe in which we live. By this definition, some might even consider the principles of physics the ultimate higher power. If this is you, that's fine. You can still benefit greatly from the ideas in this section of the book.

Second, this higher power *functions* like an organic intelligence, whether you believe it to be one or not. Just like how the activities of the neurons and thinking molecules covered in the last two sections can be mathematically quantified, analyzed, and optimized, so can the activities of subatomic particles, atoms, molecules, and all other processes in the material universe. Indeed, differences exist between these biological and material processes, and some might object to my description. But they also share many similarities, the most common one being that biological cells and chemical elements can both be examined and understood using mathematical principles and the scientific method. If you are interested in exploring it in more detail, the science of information theory is a good place to start your research. When you align the "information processes" happening in your body with the one happening in the exterior universe, you've achieved the goal of "spirituality" as defined above.

Third, and finally, the higher power produces living things fundamentally driven by the impulse to live, grow, and reproduce. And of course, death is a part of this cycle as well. But dead things are eventually absorbed back into the ground or somewhere else and can again contribute to the emergence of new life forms and the nourishment of living things.

That said, this chapter focuses on fueling your spirit for clarity, empowerment, and growth. Judgment and condemnation are more often found in religious, tribal thinking and they have no place in this book. As we align our body functions with the functions of the universe, we gain clarity about our real purpose in life and how to achieve it. The point of our inward and personal journey is to connect us with our true purpose by connecting to everything we share the universe with. Think about the concept of "real food" we discussed in the last chapter. A higher power put food into the ground for living things to eat. These living things are also food and therefore feed on each other. However, the higher power did not make Twinkies trees, potato chip plants, or rivers flowing with high-fructose corn syrup. Humans did that and we've already talked about how eating these unnatural foods will limit our ability to live a long, productive, and healthy life.

Spirituality

Connecting to a greater power with the purpose of expressing that power through our actions.

Similar principles apply to how you manage your mental states, your relationships, your habits, and your spiritual life. For instance, people are born with the basic need for trustworthy relationships. While some may have a higher need than others and everyone has different mental frameworks about how to build and retain trust, the need for trustworthy relationships itself is quite universal.

Second, the less aligned your mental frameworks are with the laws of cause and effect, the more outrageous your life will be. Just think about what would happen if you believed that driving off a cliff was a smart way to add a little excitement to your life. No matter how strongly you believed this, the law of gravity would prove you wrong. The same goes with any belief or habit that clashes with the basic laws of cause and effect.

We can choose our mental frameworks and our actions, but we don't get to choose how the laws of cause and effect determine the consequences of our actions. If we deceive people, we'll have fewer options for healthy relationships with trustworthy and positive people. If we eat fake, chemical-laden food, our odds of remaining healthy becomes slimmer as we age. If we lack confidence, adaptability, resilience, focus, and good leadership skills, we'll have dramatically fewer options for achieving our dreams than those who mastered these skills. So, a large part of this spiritual journey will be about learning to align our mental frameworks, our subconscious thought processes, our relationship skills, and our spiritual practices with the principles of the universe we live in.

The Fivefold Path to Higher Performances

In Buddhism, the "Eightfold Path" is the path to enlightenment. While some modern Buddhists are theists and consider their theistic beliefs part of their Buddhist faith, this was not in the original Buddhism doctrine. So, the Buddhist definition of Enlightenment was viable for non-spiritual pursuits and even atheists.

The idea of "the Way" or "the Path" is also found in multiple Eastern Religions, even in Early Christianity. For instance, citizens of Asia Minor and Rome called Jesus' early disciples "Followers of the Way." Some even called them "atheists" because they rejected all gods of the Greek Pantheon. The Tao Te Ching, which is the principle book of Taoism, talks many times of "the Tao," commonly translated into "the Way" In English. Meanwhile, the Chinese translation of the *New Testament Gospel of John* (Chapter One, Verses 1-8) uses the term "Tao" in place of the Greek term "Logos." In *John* 1:14, where the text speaks of Jesus Christ, the Chinese translation essentially says "…and the Tao became flesh and walked among us." These are examples of how many ancient wisdom frameworks harmonize with one another.

Don't consider these explanations as a religious lesson or a case against any specific religion. Rather, try to understand that the mental frameworks of various and seemingly disparate religions intersect ***much*** more than what modern religious fundamentalists realize or want to admit. Keep that in mind as we embark on this short but hopefully rewarding journey toward Enlightenment. We will approach this section by building a mental framework for each of the Five Capabilities by applying the definitions of spirituality in this chapter to your Five Prime Capabilities. Once we unpack these five frameworks, I'll show you how to turn them into your own and use them to achieve your highest intentions.

#1 Spiritual Confidence Through Self-Awareness

One of the oldest and most widely known spiritual proverbs is "Know yourself, and you will know the Universe and the gods."

What does this mean? It's about understanding beyond the space and time you inhabit, the titles you use (such as your name or professional title), and the roles you play (father, mother, spouse, sister, accountant, teacher, entrepreneur, etc.). It's also about moving past your own beliefs and principles, your behavior patterns, and how others perceive you. While these are all important pieces of the self-awareness puzzle, they are essentially mere extensions and expressions of your true self.

At our core, we are all beings of consciousness. As far as we know, we are capable of reaching higher capacity of thought, reason, and empathy more than any other biological lifeform. Knowing yourself means understanding what higher functionality means for your position in the cosmos. The ultimate function of living things is the expression and expansion of their intrinsic potential. Every living being will fight to the death for its right to fulfill this function.

Pour a pure cement sidewalk onto the ground. Several years later, plants eventually creep through the cracks and crevasses. Some will even break the concrete slab as their roots expand in search of water. They will seek out opportunities to express and expand their biological potential. That said, every living being has the internal impulse toward growth and expansion. They have the capability to adapt and to survive to a scope which we don't yet fully understand. This universal impulse is the will of the higher power and goes the same for you and I. Your desire to express your unique gifts and talents to the world is the will of the higher power within you seeking fulfillment.

Once you grasp and accept this simple idea, your confidence in yourself and your ability to turn your potential capabilities into realized capabilities will become unstoppable. By accepting your internal desire for greater expression of your potential, you ultimately accept that your will is aligned with the will that set the cosmos in motion. On the other hand, some people lack self-confidence because they've lost sight of this simple idea and replaced it with mental frameworks producing shame, guilt, or a sense of inferiority. Sadly, some of these people convince themselves that subordinating their dreams to other people's agendas is noble or even "holy." The need to conform to someone else's will instead of God's is where self-abasing, religious dogma came from in the first place.

It is true that if you desire to harm others, ruin their reputations, destroy their self-esteem, or take what is rightfully theirs, you should feel ashamed of such malicious thoughts. But where did these self-centered desires originate in the first place? Often, it's because these people are living in a fear-based or "survival of the fittest" mindset. As a result, they see everyone as either a prey or a predator or an opportunity to have power over another individual.

Think of all the amazing innovations in the past few hundred years. From agricultural, printing, sanitation, and medical technologies to the rapidly developing computer sciences, these inventions made everyone's life better in their pure forms. Sure, some people are so locked into the Survival Mindset that they are obsessed with gaining power over others and used these technologies to destroy, enslave, or oppress their fellow humans. But they typically act out of the fear that they must monopolize opportunities to live the life they want. Their desire is not a spiritual impulse. Rather, it's a spiritual sickness and a violation of the fundamental laws of life. Therefore, their behaviors are ultimately self-destructive. Any organism only concerned with its own survival will eventually sabotage itself. Take viruses for example. They spread until they kill their human host, then they move to a new host to keep surviving. If our immune system never fought back, the virus would eventually wipe out all potential hosts and end up destroying its opportunities to survive and thrive. Now, when our immune system, driven by our internal impulse to live and thrive, fights back despite the virus interferences, it also stops the virus's self-destructive process. This balance is found throughout nature. Without this harmonizing principle, life on this planet would be in serious trouble.

So, if your mental framework about your personal worth and the value of your abilities and dreams isn't based on this awareness, you'll want to change it right away. Let's go back to the proverb of "know yourself and you will know the gods and the universe". The sentence starts with gaining awareness of how your internal desires to express your highest potential is aligned with the higher power's will. People who lose sight of this transcendent life view eventually fall into negative mental frameworks. Fortunately, anyone, regardless of their spiritual or religious beliefs, can achieves said awareness. Even a hard-core atheist with no respect for spiritual matters can align themselves with the laws and principles governing the universe.

Think, for example, about people who compete for fame and popularity. Is this a true life purpose? Of course not. Many celebrities are secretly unhappy. Sometimes, they take their own lives because they can't handle the success or the critics that come with it. The same goes for rich people. Money is a wonderful thing and life is a lot easier when you are rich. But like any other power instruments, money can lead to self-destruction when used by someone who is not prepared to use it for benevolence. Simply imagine what would happen to a heroin addict if he were to suddenly win the lottery. This could become his death sentence knowing how he'd most likely spend the money.

There is nothing wrong with chasing fame and wealth. That is definitely not the point. However, when the majority is convinced that they need to become a rock star, a Hollywood celebrity, a sports hero, or have a huge social media following for their lives to matter, you are encouraging millions to compete against each other for the same things. This is just as abnormal as having every animal in the world competing for the same food source. Eventually, that food source will run out and the animals would starve to death.

Thankfully, nature is smarter than we are. It created a world of incredible biological diversity where millions of species depend on one another to survive. Likewise, it created a world where each person has a unique personality, and whom desires a variety of things personally and professionally. The only disruption to this balance is the false mental framework created by our society saying you must be rich, famous, powerful, beautiful (or all of these) for your life to have any meaning or value.

We must understand that every living creature has the impulse for expression and growth and our purpose is to contribute to nature's balance with our gifts, so we can make the world better for everyone.

Try to think about this familiar quote in new light:

"Thy Kingdom come, Thy will be done — on earth as it is in heaven."

Read this quote as in the higher power completes its will on earth through people like you and me. The will of heaven works through those living on the earth. A passage in the Tao Te Ching that also says:

"Humanity follows earth, earth follows heaven, heaven follows The Tao, The Tao follows only itself."

At first glance, these passages seem to contradict one another. But what does it mean for the humanity to "follow earth?" It means aligning our mental frameworks and mental states with the principles that govern the balance of life on earth, and knowing they are all expressions of the heaven or the creator's will. Ultimately, your desire to express your highest potential is the utmost noble expression of divine love. Once you grasp and accept this concept, your confidence in yourself, your dreams, and your capabilities will become unbreakable.

#2 Adaptability Through Gratitude

Can a richer spiritual life make you more adaptable? How can you train yourself to adapt to new challenges without compromising your values and who you are? Part of becoming spiritually wholesome is about reconciling the paradoxes within yourself. The most inspiring people in history are uncompromising. We admire them because they lived by their values when everyone and everything around was pushing them to surrender. However, there's a difference between resilience and simply being so stubborn that you can't adapt.

Adaptable people can change their methods without compromising their principles. For example, you can live by the principles of empathy and contribution, but still be willing to change the methods of showing empathy and contributing to others. Meanwhile, you can live by the same principles yet be so stuck in your methods that you miss opportunities to express those principles. Or you may be a conformist who changes both their methods and their principles out of fear of not being liked by others, not being enough, or not having enough. It goes back to the Growth vs. Survival Frameworks we've been talking about. Adaptability focuses on growth.

If this is not your current framework, you can change this through gratitude. You can never overstate how important gratitude is to your ability to adapt to new challenges and tap into your natural potential for creativity and innovation. First, let's look at what other authors have said about gratitude:

"Gratitude is the healthiest of all human emotions. The more you express gratitude for what you have, the more you will have to express gratitude for."

-Zig Ziglar

"The more gratefully we fix our minds on the Supreme when good things come to us, the more good things we will receive, and the more rapidly they will come; and the reason simply is that the mental attitude of gratitude draws the mind into closer touch with the source from which the blessings come."

-Wallace Wattles, *The Science of Getting Rich*

"When our vibrations are up ... we respond to stressful situations with soundness, resilience and clearer discernment. We are less vulnerable to frustration, impatience, anger, anxiety, and we feel more self-secure and less critical of others and of ourselves. We are drawn to notice nature, flowers and trees that we usually sleep-walk past, as our preoccupations rob us of this gift of conscious connection."

-Doc Childre, founder of the HeartMath Institute

Pay additional attention to the quote from the HeartMath Institute. The scientists at this institution spent years using scientific instruments to measure something they call "heart coherence." Heart coherence is when an HRV analysis shows that your heart's rhythmic patterns are more ordered and stable at a frequency of around 0.1 hertz. When you're in this state, you experience a more *"orderly and harmonious synchronization among various systems in the body such as the **heart**, respiratory system and blood-pressure rhythms."*

In other words, when you're in a state of gratitude, the heart, brain, and all other organs in your body operate in better harmony. This is the Flow State we've been talking about. However, as you can see, it's more than just your mental state. Instead, it's about all your body's thinking centers being in harmony. Researchers at the HeartMath Institute discovered that the best way to achieve this internal harmony is by practicing gratitude. The "practice" here goes beyond giving verbal thanks or visualizing the things you're grateful for. It's about keeping your brain and your body in harmony and in the state where they experience the energetic vibrations of gratitude. For clarification, here's another quote from one of the researchers at the HeartMath Institute:

> "It's important to emphasize that it is not a mental image of a memory that creates a shift in our heart rhythms," says Dr. Rollin McCraty, Director of Research. "But rather the emotions associated with the memory. Mental images alone usually do not produce the same significant results that we've observed when someone focuses on a positive feeling."

Think about how different this statement is compared to what you've read about gratitude. Most messages out there focus on thinking and visualization. Although both are important, you must do more than going through the motions to truly be grateful. You must awaken the energy of gratitude

Most of us have more capacity for innovation and strategic thinking than we realize. But we spend too much time in a state of mind and body that shuts down these natural capabilities. Remember the fight or flight nervous system responses? When we are under the survival state, our body moves blood flow away from the prefrontal cortex, which is the part of our brain that performs our higher faculties. Therefore, we also move away from our digestion, tissue repair, and other vital functions to redirect that energy toward either fighting off a perceived threat or escaping from it. But you can change this by practicing gratitude.

#3 Resilience Through Faith and Hope

Spiritual people often talk about having faith. But where you put your faith has a lot to do with how useful and consistent your faith is. Hebrews 11:1 says:

"Now faith is confidence in what we hope for and assurance about what we do not see."

To me, this means having trust in God's plan for our life, while understanding that a man has free will and is fully responsible for his actions. God may have a plan for our life, but the choices are still ours and therefore we are never off the hook and we should always take responsibility for our lives. Your choices and actions are your responsibilities.

This definition of faith also has something to teach those who don't believe in the traditional God or a higher power at all. Here, faith stands for believing in a hopeful future outcome based on your understanding of the natural principles of cause and effect. Of course, no one knows everything about those principles especially when it comes to the future. But the more clarity we have about our capabilities and expectations, the more we can be certain of a desired outcome. For example, I'm certain that if I practice a foreign language for one hour every day consistently for twelve months, I could learn to have a decent conversation with someone in that language. If I keep this up for five years, I'm certain that I'll be able to have more complex conversations. If I keep this up for ten years, I'm certain that I'd become fluent in that language. I'm also certain that if I worked with a language coach once a week, on top of my daily practice, I could increase my chances of succeeding faster. Am I predicting the future? Not really. I'm simply applying some basic common-sense principles about how the human mind learns over time.

You might be wondering what this has to do with resilience. First, we need to differentiate physical and mental/emotional resilience. Physical resilience comes from practicing the principles we talked about in the "Body Fuel" section. It is also the foundation for your mental and emotional resilience. If you don't train yourself to be physically resilient, it will be hard to reach mental and emotional resilience. Remember, your brain uses approximately a quarter of your daily caloric energy. Suppose you're out of shape or are suffering chronic inflammation, poor gut health, or an unbalanced endocrine system, you'll have a lot less mental and emotional energy to apply toward recovering from failures and disappointments.

It's indeed crucial to challenge the common assumptions about people's capabilities to understand resilience. After all, Roger Bannister did run the four-minute mile despite everyone insisting it was biologically impossible. However, he didn't just hop up off the couch, set down his beer and chips, and run his first mile in four minutes. He constantly pushed his limits, failed, recovered, all the while rethinking his approach and developing self-awareness by exploring his physical and mental capabilities. As a result, he kept expanding his limits. By the time he set out to run the four-minute mile, he'd developed a wealth of knowledge about himself and the art and science of running. When it's time to challenge the mental frameworks of his peers, he summoned all his knowledge and experience and blew away the expectations of those who lacked the self-awareness he so diligently earned. In other words, his hope was not based on ignorance but on his knowledge and experience about his body's performance potential and biological limitations. It was only after he had found his natural rhythm that he pushed the envelope and changed the perception of what was possible.

To put this into a spiritual context, think about the story of Jesus of Nazareth. He spent years training his disciples before commissioning them to spread his message after he was gone. Their faith was based on the knowledge and experience gained during this training, not on blind hope. Likewise, Siddhartha Gautama, the founder of Buddhism, learned many lessons before he finally discovered the Eightfold Path to Enlightenment and put his faith in it. Nearly every spiritual tradition requires a vast amount of preparation, tribulation, and learning before putting any trust in the learnings.

Otherwise, the students would be setting themselves up for epic disappointments once they realized that their ignorance had caused them to put their faith in things that defied their creator's will. Does this sound like spiritual babbling to you? If so, let's finish up with a statement from Thomas G. Plante, Ph.D., ABPP, a psychologist and the editor of the American Psychological Association's professional journal, *Spirituality in Clinical Practice*.

> "There seems to be a growing expectation that we should be able to secure the perfect spouse, the perfect career, the perfect home, engineer the perfect children, so forth, to be happy. If this doesn't happen, according to our plans, then something is wrong that needs fixing or somehow we are ashamed of our performance and let it affect our overall physiological status. While we all likely believe that we should have high expectations for ourselves, unrealistically high expectations can become counterproductive and destructive.[xxx]"

Some may accuse Dr. Plante and myself, of telling people to lower their standards. However, we are simply asking everyone to manage expectations wisely. Think again about our example of Roger Bannister and the four-minute mile. Your ability to manage expectations has a tremendous impact on your ability to persevere. If your expectations are based on knowledge and experience of your unrealized potential and your biological limitations, these expectation frameworks will be much more stable. We all rolled over in the crib a few times before we could crawl, walk, and eventually run. Likewise, the more you practice the ideas in this book, the more clarity you'll have about your capabilities *and* how the basic laws of human development and cause and effect drive the results. In time, with patience, you can upgrade your hopes and allow your faith to mature naturally. This is the path to resilience and happiness. On the other hand, people who can't do this have a hard time starting small or remaining consistent until they build up enough momentum to succeed big.

There's a simple line in a song by Chumbawamba that me and my family loves for many reasons: "I get knocked down, but I get up again. They're never gonna keep me down."

No matter how hard life hits, you got to hit back much harder. But before you can do that, you must get up first. If your hopes are not grounded in the growth-based mental framework featured in this book, it will be much more difficult to get up and you may often feel it's not even worth trying to get back on your feet.

However, failure doesn't overtake you when you fail. It only overtakes you when you give up instead of adjusting your approach and pressing forward. Our worst failures come when we don't learn from them, and the highest form of learning is discovering whether our personal values and choices align with the higher power. Everything in life is temporary. If you want to move forward, you must choose to do so.

Many successful individuals talk about failing forward. That's because if you're not failing, you're not pushing your boundaries and therefore are not growing. To achieve all that you want in life, you must be able to employ a system that pushes you forward and pivots where needed. Failure can be the bedrock of your future masterpiece if you're able to learn from each situation and take that learning into your next mission.

My inability to build momentum and be my most resilient when I failed in a past endeavor, was one of the reasons that inspired me to write this book. I needed new mental frameworks and methods of managing my own expectations. This took me on a journey that sparked a desire to improve my ability to deliver what I feel is the most important information in the world, the information to perform at optimal levels. As I continued to learn the importance of writing and how it can influence the learning process, it turned into a beautiful challenge of transferring this energy through words. I could only hope to provide some insights by sharing these learnings. Similarly, when you choose not to fear rejection or failure, and instead decide to have courage, get out of your comfort zone, and pursue growth,

1. Your self-esteem grows to new heights (confidence).
2. You become stronger-willed (more resilient).
3. You become more efficient at winning (adaptability).
4. You refine your goals and your methods (focus).
5. You inspire others to follow your example (leadership).

You've got to learn to be tough to persevere in this chaotic world. However, if your current road seems full of resistance, you may want to redirect your path. Get out of your comfort zone, unstick yourself from emotions, and face your fears of failing again. Build the necessary courage and expose yourself to new things and ideas, so that every time you fail, you fail forward.

In addition, see the value behind small beginnings and slow but steady progress. Small, consistent actions will beat massive sporadic actions anytime with their cumulative effects.

Think about Jesus' parable about the mustard seed, an analogy about the relationship between faith, hope, expectations, and resilience:

> "The kingdom of heaven is like a mustard seed, which a man took and planted in his field. Though it is the smallest of all seeds, yet when it grows, it is the largest of garden plants and becomes a tree, so that the birds come and perch in its branches."

If you start ***any*** journey with the expectation that an idea's seed will grow into something truly momentous, you will find your faith invincible and your resilience unbreakable.

#4 Mindfulness – The Key to Clarity and Focus

I highly appreciated one unique aspect in Buddhism and all other eastern religions, the practice of meditation and mindfulness. Since the concept of mindfulness came from the east, we'll start with those traditions before looking into the science behind them. In Buddhism, the first two verses of the first chapter of The Dhammapada say:

> "All that we are is the result of what we have thought: it is founded on our thoughts, it is made up of our thoughts. If a man speaks or acts with an evil thought, pain follows him, as the wheel follows the foot of the ox that draws the carriage... if a man speaks or acts with a pure thought, happiness follows him, like a shadow that never leaves him."

These words tell us that where we focus our thoughts determines who we become and how we experience life. This statement is consistent with our knowledge on the human mind and the body of evidence is growing every year. We talked about neuroplasticity, the brain's ability to change itself according to habitual thoughts earlier in this book. Several years before I wrote that chapter, Dalai Lama visited the United States and gave a speech about meditation and mindfulness at The Society for Neuroscience's annual meeting in Washington D.C. He'd been helping recruit Tibetan Buddhist monks to aid studies on meditation and its impact on the brain. These studies took place at the Waisman Laboratory for Brain Imaging and Behavior at the University of Wisconsin-Madison. The results suggested that people who had practiced meditation for at least a decade or longer had altered their brains' structure and function through neuroplasticity. These studies' details are available online, but this quote should give you a brief idea of what the researchers found:

- "Such changes include alterations in patterns of brain function assessed with functional magnetic resonance imaging (fMRI), changes in the cortical evoked response to visual stimuli that reflect the impact of meditation on attention, and alterations in amplitude and synchrony of high frequency oscillations that probably play an important role in connectivity among widespread circuitry in the brain.[xxxi]"

Earlier in this book, we talked about how the only difference between thinking signals transferred between neurons was their individual frequency. Here, the high frequency oscillations allow you to enter the Flow State. These studies found that meditation can strengthen your brain's ability to generate high frequency signals. This is exactly what the Buddhists have been telling us for centuries. To put this idea into perspective, let's look at more verses from The Dhammapada (Book Two). Notice how the author uses the word "earnestness."

21. Earnestness is the path of immortality (Nirvana), thoughtlessness the path of death. Those who are in earnest do not die, those who are thoughtless are as if dead already.

22. Those who are advanced in earnestness, having understood this clearly, delight in earnestness, and rejoice in the knowledge of the Ariyas (the elect).

23. These wise people, meditative, steady, always possessed of strong powers, attain to Nirvana, the highest happiness.

(*From the F Max Muller Translation)

The modern meaning of the word earnest is "a sincere and intense conviction." But in Buddhism and other eastern religions, earnestness includes the mind's intense and sincere focus on a particular object or idea. By practicing earnestness, we develop some of our most sincere and intense convictions. In other words, earnestness is the tangible method that turns ideas into mental frameworks through neuroplasticity. It is found throughout ancient spiritual texts, such as Book Three of *The Yoga Sutras of Patanjali*, one of the most important literatures to understand Raja Yoga's practice and benefits. Here, practicing mindful meditation is described in even more details.

Verse One: The binding of the perceiving consciousness to a certain region is attention (dharana).

Verse Two: A prolonged holding of the perceiving consciousness in that region is meditation (dhyana).

Verse Three: When the perceiving consciousness in this meditative is wholly given to illuminating the essential meaning of the object contemplated and is freed from the sense of separateness and personality, this is contemplation (samadhi).

Verse Four: When these three, attention, meditation contemplation, are exercised at once, this is perfectly concentrated meditation (sanyama).

Verse Five: By mastering this perfectly concentrated meditation, there comes the illumination of perception.

Notice the simple progression. Verse One's instruction asks us to focus on a "certain region." Then, we hold that focus (Verse Two) with earnestness until the object of focus consumes our consciousness (Verse Three). Combine these three practices to form the "perfectly concentrated meditation" and reach the "illumination of perception" (Verse Four & Five). What does the perfectly concentrated meditation do for your mind and your body? Let's look at some later verses in Book Three of the Yoga Sutras and find out (notice my emphasis in *italics*).

Verse Twenty-Nine: Perfectly concentrated meditation on *the center of force in the lower trunk* brings *an understanding of the order of the bodily powers.*

Verse Thirty: By perfectly concentrated meditation on the *center of force in the well of the throat*, there comes the *cessation of hunger and thirst.*

Verse Thirty-One: By perfectly concentrated meditation on the *center of force in the channel called the 'tortoise-formed,'* comes steadfastness.

Verse Thirty-Two: Through perfectly concentrated meditation on the *light in the head* comes the vision of the masters who have attained.

Remember what I said in the Body Fuel section about the gut-brain and your messenger molecules? Verse Twenty-Nine talks about if we meditate on this region, we can gain "understanding (control and clarity)" about the "orders of the bodily powers," referring to the digestive system and its complementary organs. Remember, nerve cells are everywhere in your body, including in your gut. How does this relate to the study on meditation and neuroplasticity? Verse Thirty refers to the "center of force in the well of your throat" and the "cessation of hunger or thirst." This is a reference to the thyroid gland and its control over your metabolism and your ability to control and regulate your appetite. The "tortoise-formed" channel mentioned in Verse Thirty-One refers to the upper chest region where the thymus gland that maintains a healthy immune system can be found. Apparently, this is what "steadfastness" was referring to. Or, as we call it in this book, resilience. Finally, in verse Thirty-Two, the "light in the head" clearly refers to the pineal gland we mentioned in the previous chapter.

These verses were written hundreds of years ago, yet the author understood the concept of our body having multiple thought centers and that these centers were controllable by deliberately training your mind through meditation. This is more than spiritual speculation. Plenty of scientific evidence will back this concept up. For example, here's a statement from Dr. Daniel Siegal[xxxii] confirming the ability to direct neuron development through neuroplasticity, using mindful meditation.

> "How attention directs that flow will activate certain neural pathways and activate certain interpersonal experiences. Within us, attention drives the activation of neurons in the brain, at a minimum. Perhaps this inner attention drives energy flow throughout the whole body.

> When we communicate with one another, too, as I write and you read these words, we are also harnessing the power of attention to direct the flow of energy and its symbolic forms we call information. Energy and information flow between us as well as within us. With shifts in neural activation, the opportunity to change the structure of the brain is created. With shifts in external attention, the opportunity is created to alter the internal neural firings that shape not only the activity in the brain in the moment, but also alter the structural connections in the brains of those engaged in the interactions, in the communication, among people in the world. What this suggests is that the mind, within and between, can change the structure of the brain."

Personally, I find this fascinating. I've always known that we have malleable minds at some level, but the more I've researched, the more I'm blown away by the power we have over our minds. Ancient spiritual practitioners thousands of years ago foretold the scientific discoveries we've only made in the last five decades. That ought to be enough to inspire you to take these suggestions seriously and start practicing mindful meditation because the more you meditate, the more you develop your ability to focus on training your mind and body to serve you, instead of manipulate you.

Now, let's revisit Buddhism and look at a few more verses on thoughts from the third book of *The Dhammapada.*

35. It is good to tame the mind, which is difficult to hold in and flighty, rushing wherever it listeth; a tamed mind brings happiness.

36. Let the wise man guard his thoughts, for they are difficult to perceive, very artful, and they rush wherever they list: thoughts well-guarded bring happiness.

37. Those who bridle their mind which travels far, moves about alone, is without a body, and hides in the chamber (of the heart), will be free from the bonds of Mâra (the tempter).

38. If a man's thoughts are unsteady, if he does not know the true law, if his peace of mind is troubled, his knowledge will never be perfect.

39. If a man's thoughts are not dissipated, if his mind is not perplexed, if he has ceased to think of good or evil, then there is no fear for him while he is watchful.

Notice how Verse Thirty-Nine says, "then there is no fear for him while he is watchful". And think about how this relates to the Growth vs. Survival Mindset conversation we've been having throughout this book. The verse tells us that taming the mind through mindful meditation is the path out of fear and all the above examples direct back to the introduction that defined spirituality as "connecting to a greater power with the purpose of expressing that power through our actions."

What does it mean to "express that power through your actions?" This quote, used to begin this chapter, will give you the answer:

"What we commonly call man, the eating, drinking, planting, counting man, does not, as we know him, represent himself, but misrepresents himself. Him we do not respect, but the soul, whose organ he is, would he let it appear through his action, would make our knees bend."

-Ralph Waldo Emerson, *The Oversoul*

In conclusion, mindful mediation is the "bridge" between the higher power and our body, which is a thinking organism. We use mindful meditation to train our minds and bodies to obey the higher power's will. This idea is also seen in Western religions. Therefore, I'll finish this section with a passage from the New Testament:

"Do not conform to the pattern of this world, but be transformed by the renewing of your mind. Then you will be able to test and approve what God's will is--his good, pleasing and perfect will."

-Romans 12:2

Regardless of Paul's original meaning in this passage, we now know that the mind can be "renewed" and thus transform ourselves into whom we have the potential to become. Modern science, eastern, and western spiritual traditions all agree on this matter. Therefore, now it's simply a question of putting it into tangible practice. You must understand that I'm not some marathon meditator who practices these techniques every day in thirty-to-ninety-minute sessions. For most of us, there is no need to do so either. In fact, ten-to-fifteen-minute meditation sessions several days a week would bring you tremendous benefits. The more vital factor is how intentional your focus is when you meditate and how you must consistently train that focus so it turns into a habit. Once you've started this simple practice, you're ready for the most rewarding spiritual experience in this world.

#5 Leadership and the Consciousness Quality

What do Jesus of Nazareth, Siddhartha Gautama, and Mahatma Gandhi all have in common besides being some of the most influential leaders in human history? They've all been highly enlightened and brought magnificent contributions to humanity. And they were all brilliant leaders who shared their path and knowledge so more could become enlightened.

So, what does it mean to be enlightened? Let's start with the definition:

Enlightenment

When your mental frameworks, mental state, body intelligence, and spiritual consciousness arealigned with the principles that drive the laws of cause and effect in the universe.

Now, add a drive to use your enlightened state to make the world a better place for everyone and you have the definition of enlightened contributions. Of course, this is not an all or nothing definition. There are different degrees of enlightenment and that level rises and falls as your life unfolds. However, ultimately, enlightenment starts with wholesomeness. The more wholesome you are, the more often you'll be able to live in an enlightened state. Enlightened people are not in conflict with themselves. They're not riddled with shame, fear, or guilt. They're not held captive by their positive emotions like pleasure or pride either. They still experience negative emotions and are tightly connected to their positive emotions as well. However, they are not ruled by them. Instead, wholesome people's mind, body, and soul all work in harmony. Enlightened contributors are the best leaders because they've blended personal wholeness with a desire to give. When you're in conflict with yourself, you're not whole but instead, indecisive. Meanwhile, no one wants to follow a leader who is uncertain in their perception, thoughts, actions, and directions.

Moreover, ancient and modern shamans believe all illnesses, physical and mental, are spiritual in nature. It's easy to think of this idea as mere ignorance and superstition. But if you consider what we just covered about the harmony between ancient spiritual teachings and modern neuroscience, the sages of the past surely deserve to be taken seriously. If you've ever struggled to maintain optimal mental health, you may relate to this. Your hope would be to become whole in mind and body by using the practices we just discussed.

Remember what I said earlier about cognitive dissonance?

Cognitive dissonance happens when your body warns you about a conflict in your thought patterns or between your mental frameworks and the reality. This conflict leads to worry, worry leads to doubt, and doubt crystalizes into fear, unless you find a way to shift out of this debilitating mindset and move into a more powerful mental framework about yourself and your dreams. In other words, you must practice self-awareness. Wholesome people are *self-aware*, whereas *self-conscious* people desperately seek approval from others. If you care so much about what others think and what they have that you don't, you're setting yourself up for a brutal life. To thrive, you must become bulletproof to criticism and do what you need to do. If people don't like it, so be it. If they continue to criticize you, they're not the kind of people you should surround yourself with.

Nowadays, many people talk about the role of consciousness in achieving enlightenment. But what the heck is consciousness and how do you increase its quality? Earlier in this book, we mentioned that the signals sent by your neurons are identical in every aspect except for their frequencies. We also mentioned how the frequency is the only difference between how you experience a paper cut and a chainsaw amputation. The same applies with every thought impulse that takes place in your body, whether triggered by a sound, a smell, a taste, a visual stimulus, or an emotion. Frequency defines different conscious experiences between your seemingly infinite array of consciousness experiences.

In other words, consciousness functions as "slices" of film scenes or the "bits" and "frames" of an audio recording.

Therefore, let's look at the differences between high and low-quality movie productions and audio recordings. The frequency of these conscious slices determines your experience and your perception's quality the same way a film's frame rate the image and sound quality of the movie you're watching. Notice how old black and white films look grainy and jerky sometimes? This is because these older films had a lower frame rate. Likewise, old audio recordings sounded poor even if they might be high-quality back then, because they were recorded at a lower sampling rate. As film frame rates grew, the visual quality of films also increased. As the sampling rates increased, the sound quality of the music we listen to has gone up as well. Likewise, when you increase the frequency of your conscious moments, your experience of reality becomes more vivid and you increase your clarity significantly. This is a scientifically corroborated model for how consciousness works in your body. In general, the frequency of thought impulses in your nervous system defines the quality of your conscious experience.

So, what meaning does this model have regarding becoming a better leader? Let's get back to our definition of enlightenment:

"Enlightenment happens when your **mental frameworks,** your **mental state**, your **body intelligence**, and your **spiritual consciousness** are aligned with the principles that drive the laws of cause and effect in the universe."

We talked about mental frameworks and your mental state

in the Brain Fuel section. We also discussed your physiological state in the Body Fuel section. Thus, our last task is aligning your consciousness with reality by increasing the frequency of your consciousness moments. The better you can increase the frequency, the more clarity you will gain about reality *and* your internal vision of that reality. The same mathematical laws that allow this to happen have also allowed us to create more vivid experiences in film and music.

In his book *The Speed of Trust,* Stephen MR Covey (son of Stephen R Covey) said that a leader's first job is to define reality. Well, he's right. After all, you can't make the vision in your mind real if you don't understand where you are or the resources you have that would make it come true. Besides, the higher your perception quality, the more successful you'll be at defining reality. In return, you will become a better leader.

Next, you need a vision of where you and your team are going. You must clearly visualize the end destination in your mind's eye that the visualization mutes all external noises so you can truly focus. Then, you must have the adaptability and resilience required to adjust your methods without compromising your vision, and to continue to push forward until your visions come true.

These three factors become your second nature as you improve the quality of your perception. While this is not as complicated as many think, it's also not that easy. The texts we've talked about in this section were clearly written by people who have been exploring this practice for years. Astoundingly, they somehow knew these things long before we had the scientific tools to validate their opinions, and that's what makes these ancient sages the best leaders for us to follow, even today.

Since we've made your spiritual growth a solid case with a wide collection of ancient wisdom and modern science, I'd like to share my personal convictions on this matter. I understand some readers might consider this next section "too religious." Therefore, you're free to skip it if you like. However, I'm including this short section for those who are curious about my personal perspective on God and on our relationship with our creator.

The Hope of Heaven

There is an age-old hope that after our journey is over here, we will have more opportunities to learn, contribute, and grow in the afterlife. To some of you, this might not matter as much. But for thousands of years, mankind has been obsessed with the idea of a life after death and we should not be so quick to dismiss the whole idea as a primitive superstition. If it turns out that we truly are beings of pure consciousness, then an afterlife is not only possible but highly probable.

Every material structure in the universe from atoms to molecules, DNA, and the planetary bodies and galaxies is the product of an information process. As far as we know, the most organized information processes in the known universe are happening inside your body right now. In other words, we are the products of consciousness — of spirit.

It's perfectly reasonable to believe that the spirit is the source of everything and that we all have a piece of the higher power living in us. Those who believe that spirits can survive after the death of our material body, which is when the way our bodily matter is organized changes, have a supernatural amount of confidence and courage in their purpose on earth.

This is the hope of heaven. To deny its existence is, in a sense, to deny who we really are. As a Christian, I will quote the Gospel of John (Verse 14) as my evidence:

“The Word became flesh and made his dwelling among us. We have seen his glory, the glory of the one and only Son, who came from the Father, full of grace and truth.”

This verse speaks about the incarnation of the one universal spirit into a flesh and blood body. This was the birth of Jesus Christ. Later, his body was offered a willing sacrifice to the higher power, which Jesus called “The Father”. Then, Jesus proved that he was who he claimed to be by conquering death and ascending into heaven to reunite with the Father. Through this process, He showed us a way to do the same. Therefore, the hope of heaven is the hope that we can follow this path ourselves. To live with the hope of heaven is, I believe, the beginning of creating heaven on earth.

My hope of heaven is also rooted in the hope that I will get to see the loved ones that I’ve lost along the way. There’s unfortunately a few of them already and I can’t wait to see them again.

From Mindfulness to Momentum

We described momentum as the Master Capability earlier. So far, we’ve aimed to achieve your peak performance state by turning your daily actions into habits. By harmonizing your brain, body and spirit toward conscious actions, you’ll start the process to creating momentum in your pursuits. The more mindful and aware you become on this journey, the more present you will become and you'll see opportunities and relationships attract themselves to you, more often.

Mindfulness is also how you maintain your personal momentum and add to it, while minimizing other's ability to overtake your journey by negativity, their limited world view, or their attempt to shrink your ambitions. This is more than about people who try to bring you down. Even those who love you or work with you will never see your vision as clearly as you do. Because that's not their job. It's yours. Thus, mindfulness becomes essential if you want to transition from self-leadership to social leadership, and turn your private victories into shared ones. A mindful person sees their internal vision so clearly, vividly, and steadfastly that no exterior influence can penetrate their consciousness and reduce, confuse, or contaminate that vision.

Indeed, you should always be open to positive influence to refine your vision and plans. That is a quality all good leaders have. Nonetheless, you should be accepting and denying outside influences on your own terms so that you insulate yourself from distractions, both good and bad ones, without isolating yourself from those who can help you, hold you accountable, or encourage you to press on in the face of hardship and failures. Finally, cultivate the practice of mindfulness in your private time, and you'll be even more prepared for what we're going to cover next.

CHAPTER 7: SOCIAL FUEL

"Alone we can do so little, together we can do so much."

-Helen Keller

"At the end of the day it's not about what you have or even what you've accomplished... It's about who you've lifted up, who you've made better. It's about what you've given back."

-Denzel Washington

"Talent wins games, but teamwork and intelligence wins championships."

-Michael Jordan

The most powerful and persevering capability fuel comes from your personal and professional networks. We humans need social interaction for optimal health. Communication is changing in our technologically shifting world and so is the need for effective social fuels. With this, it's natural for us to follow tribal or social groups as we age because it can be healthy for our survival. Anyone that chooses to pave their own path, especially against a norm, is making a choice that will require additional fuels and capabilities that can help them withstand the friction of going against the grain. The more you learn to handle these independent journeys, the more you'll develop the capabilities to level up and power through them. Therefore, learning how to build and master your social fuels, will propel your personal and social journey most effectively.

When people cheer you on, your capabilities are amplified. You become more empathetic, confident, and communicative. The sheer power of positive Social Fuel magnifies all your existing knowledge and capabilities, and continues to feed back into those around you, and then comes back to you, again, multiplied. The more this cycle happens, the more impact you have on those around you. I call this Social Leadership, the power that brings synergy into your life. It's how 1+1=3 (or 4 or 5). This is part of Stephen Covey's Habit #6 (Synergize) from *7 Habits of Highly Effective People*. Synergization is referenced as the miracle habit, because this is where individual powers and energies combine to create something far greater than the individual can create on their own.

Let's revisit the basics first. Social Leadership starts with Self-Leadership. We covered the Brain Fuel, Body Fuel, and Spirit Fuel sections first because they help you build self-awareness, foster discipline, and fuel your Five Prime Capabilities in your personal life, so you can now combine those strategies and use Self-Leadership as a leverage to create Social Leadership. Meanwhile, disregarding information in the first few sections will create obstacles before moving forward with the final section, because Self-Leadership is all about taking charge of your "locus of control." Locus of control is the degree to which you control the conditions of your life and your responses to those conditions. People with a low locus of control are heavily influenced by external forces like other peoples' opinions, manipulations or the pressure of failing or succeeding. You become more vulnerable to external forces such as failure, disappointment, or toxic behaviors and individuals.

Meanwhile, certain practices can help you draw your locus of control inward. The more internal and self-influenced it becomes, the more adept you'll become at social leadership. This is how you become someone who radiates *and* receives positive energy and makes a profound and lasting impact on other people even after you're gone. Believe me, I understand how big of a promise this is. In this section, I will lay out some simple actions to practice Social Leadership. Then, we'll conclude with a plan for turning those actions into habits. We're going to focus on progress and taking things one practical step at a time.

Think about how houses are built. For a finished product to look amazing, a significant amount of time, energy, money, and specialized knowledge must go into the project. With the right training and resources, you and I could build a house from the foundation up because, like everything else that's ever built, building a house also follows a certain process. Like all other processes, building a house can also be broken down into smaller, simpler, and more teachable steps. From mixing and pouring the foundation, to plumbing, electric, woodworking, insulation, and drywall, they are a collection of individual actions performed by people like us and together they form the house-building process. This process has been successfully followed millions of times and the proof is all around us. In other words, all it takes to build a house yourself is the motivation to learn and some basic capabilities. The same goes for building a solid circle of positive people and fortifying your life against negative influences.

Start with reflecting on the Brain Fuel, Body Fuel, and Spirit Fuel sections one more time. It's nearly impossible to build and sustain a healthy social life without getting your brain, body, and spiritual life together first. This will become clearer as we unpack the ideas in this section.

Don't assume the suggestions in this section will "not work." Also, don't deny yourself the possibility to apply these suggestions simply because you're shy or an introverted person. Introverts have unique natural advantages[xxxiii] when it comes to social interactions. They are observant and are naturally good listeners. In most cases, introverts think before they speak. If you don't believe these are advantages, think about how important it is to listen with the intent to understand instead of the intent to respond. I'm not saying extroverts can't learn these listening skills, but they don't have the natural aptitude introverts do when it comes to listening. Therefore, being an introvert doesn't put you at a disadvantage in practicing and even mastering Social Leadership.

Social Fuel is just as much about fueling others as it is fueling yourself. Consider the "furnace vs. generator" metaphor we used earlier in this book. Furnaces only burn energy, whereas generators can serve as an energy *source*. The same goes for Social Fuels. For instance, if my primary mission in life is to be a generator for the people around me, I'd want all my Brain,

Body, and Spirit Fuels to empower me to radiate positive energy and influence on everyone I allowed into my circle of influence. Notice I use the word "allow" here. This is critical because sometimes you meet people who are more like furnaces than generators. They suck energy from other people, burn it up, and repeat this process until their relationships become completely dry. Then they move on to find other victims. Therefore, not only is it important to not become one of these vampires, but it's just as important to keep their influence away from you and prohibit them from entering your circle.

That said, my mission is to help you build a mental framework and a set of habits that will make you a magnet for positive, emotionally healthy people, while protecting you from the influence of those who only bring you and your circle down. With the right Social Fuel, you can unstuck yourself and build unstoppable momentum in ALL dimensions of your life.

Trust Walls and Influence Gates

Trust is essential for building positive relationships. It determines who we allow to influence us and whether they remain long-term influences throughout our lives. It also determines who we give access to the most personal parts of our life and our professional endeavors. Simply put, trust is how we open our lives to others' influence. Your ability to trust those around you determines what kind of energy you receive from your social network. Your ability to influence, on the other hand, determines what kind of energy other people receive from you.

Let's begin with a mental framework designed to help you

radiate and receive positive energy while guarding your life against negativities. This is your "social palace." As we mentioned earlier, your social palace is fortified against negative and dangerous influences but welcomes healthy and positive ones. In other words, you will build a wall around your social palace while adding gates through which positive people pass. This expanded framework is called the "Trust Wall and Influence Gates." While your trust wall keeps toxic people out, your influence gates allow positive individuals in so they can bring good influence on your life. It's not a bad thing to put up walls and keep people out so long that you build gates to let people through and you manage them wisely. Practically speaking, almost everyone you meet comes with their own walls and that's not a bad thing at all. The question is whether you have the social capabilities to persuade them to invite you into *their* social palace.

The second question is how immune you can make yourself to negative influences from others. There's a Biblical proverb that goes like this: *"like a city whose walls are broken through is a person who lacks self-control. (Proverbs 25:28)"* It beautifully fits into the concept of Self Leadership and Social Leadership. Think back to your locus of control and what we said about how people who practice Self-Leadership are less vulnerable to negative influences because they know who to invite into their lives following healthy boundaries. Meanwhile, people with an *external* locus of control are more vulnerable to criticism, disapproval, and other negative influences. They haven't developed the ability to extend what Stephen Covey calls the "Smart Trust". Let's dive into the power of building trust, to change lives and impact organizations. Trust is a fundamental power that when extended, creates opportunities for those who embody it. If you build this Smart Trust, you'll attract opportunities and impactful people into your life. In an unpredictable marketplace that is low in trust, building Smart Trust increases your probability of positive outcomes. Otherwise, social palaces would be vulnerable to invasions from toxic or manipulative people. They would be cities with broken walls.

Nonetheless, we're all a little sloppy in managing our trust gates. Think about how much trust we extend to others out of convenience or sometimes desperation. For example, when you board a plane, you're trusting the pilot whom you've most likely never met in your life. That's a big investment. You're also trusting the mechanics who checked the plane and approved the takeoff, the engineers who designed the plane, and the riveters who tightened the wings. In this case, we don't have the time or the energy to verify whether a person is trustworthy. So instead, we extend trust to perfect strangers. Other times, we extend trust out of desperation, for example, when we allow someone known to be toxic or abusive back into your life because you "need" their company, affection, or attention. Your instincts tell you that these people aren't trustworthy, but you let them in regardless for the sake of convenience or due to a lack of discipline. Just like that, we forfeit our trust skills and make decisions whose outcomes may not be good for us. When we make decisions like this, we are responding to the Survival Mindset while allowing desperation and laziness to take control.

Therefore, it's critical to ensure that your trust walls aren't broken, and your influence gates can't be opened by anyone. Luckily, you don't need to check the walls and gates out of fear while in Survival Mindset. In fact, the more confident, resilient, and focused you are, the better you become at adapting to new circumstances without compromising your values. This will make you more effective at attracting the right people and repelling toxic ones. Growth Mindsets attract growth mindsets, and vice versa. Are you starting to see why we started with the sections on Self Leadership before moving on to discussing Social Leadership?

The social palace framework will also help you better understand people in personal and professional settings and determine how they manage their own social palaces. Some people have thicker trust walls while others have almost no walls at all. Some people enter new relationships with their influence gates wide open, while others come in with their influence gates shut but still unlocked. Then, you have people who show up with their gate locked, dead bolted, and are set with armed guards and attack dogs.

So, which group do you belong to?

Remember, there is no right or wrong answer, so be honest with your responses. It's better to understand where you are than lying to yourself. It's also a good idea to understand where other people are regarding their assumptions on how, when, and why to trust someone. Most importantly, we should never assume that others manage their social palaces the same way we do. As we age, one of the vital facts we learn is that others rarely think like you do. People have different perceptions and experiences that led them to having different frameworks and belief systems. It's easy to forget this and project our own beliefs and behaviors onto them when we are not paying enough attention and practicing mindfulness.

For instance, if you lead with open gates, you may be tempted to assume that other people should do the same. This attitude won't get you far with someone who puts heavy guards on their gates. If you want to influence them, you need to start from their frame of reference. I can tell you from life experience that people with thick trust walls and heavily guarded gates have their reasons and it's wrong to assume those reasons to be invalid. In fact, people who demand trust right away may not be so good at earning trust via actions.

Now, how do you convince someone to open their influence gates? How do you know when it's smart to open yours or to close them to keep a negative person out? You've probably known people who get into bad relationships and stay that way because they don't know when to shut their gates to someone taking advantage of them. You've probably also known people who opened their gates too quickly to others and then slammed them shut just as fast. Maybe you've been in one or both of these situations yourself. Regardless, our goal in this section is to use this mental framework to manage your relationships with the right amount of trust and the right amount of influence. In conclusion:

Trust determines when and how to open *your* gates.

Influence is how you inspire someone to open *their* gates.

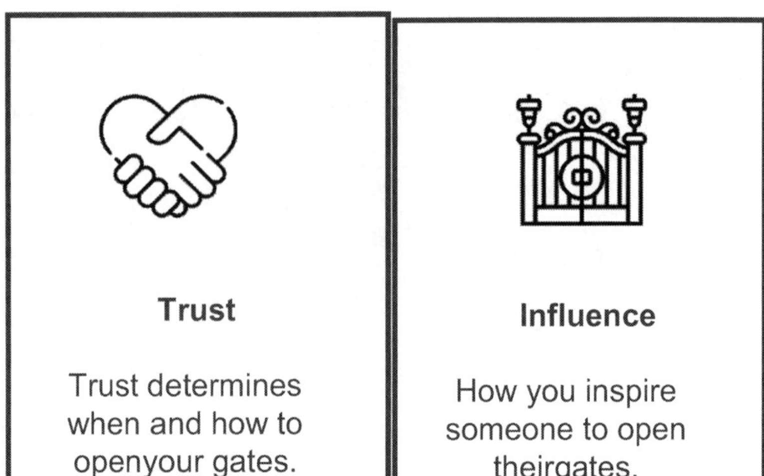

With the appropriate balance and fortitude, you will become an influential person and an inspiring leader. This model can also help you build and inspire a culture of winning and making progress if you are leading a team or a company. After all, leadership is all about gaining trust and radiating influence. If you're a "Social Generator" who consistently radiates trust and influence, very few limits will restrict you from building and leading a positive and powerful team or organization.

The First Principle of Leadership

The first principle of Social Leadership is understanding who you're talking to and what drives them. If you interact with everyone the same way, you'll only be able to understand and influence a small number of people.

What does it mean to know who you're talking to? First,

you must understand the potential impact they could have on your life. This teaches you a lot on how to interact with them. I'm going to borrow a simple model from Dr. Verna Price's book *The Power of People* to put this into perspective.

#1 - Adders can bring positive vibes into a relationship, whether it's by being a good friend or a part of your support system throughout your life journey. They add to your life and therefore you should invest your energy into building relationships with individuals like this.

#2 - Subtractors pull you down and bring mostly negative vibes your way. People with this type of attitude can drain your energy and sometimes deter you from your goals. Steer clear of giving your time to these types of people or your mind might be affected by their negative influence.

#3 - Multipliers multiply the resources and connections they bring into your life. When my life is done, I hope people will remember me as a multiplier. These individuals take pride in helping others succeed, whether directly or indirectly. Attaching yourself to multipliers will serve you many times over. Do what you need to, to provide them with something beneficial while leveraging their service to make your journey much more fruitful and rewarding.

#4 - Dividers want nothing good for anyone. They're obsessed with control and see everyone as either a prey to be conquered or a predator to be eliminated. They may even appear friendly at first. In the back, they talk badly about you to others. They see other people's happiness as a threat to their own unhappiness and are out to make everyone as miserable as they are. They're the type of people who will sabotage others for their own benefit or at the very least, to limit yours. Their intention is to keep you stuck so you never outperform them. Unfortunately, you will meet many of these people throughout your journey and it's vital to not waste any time on them.

Knowing which type you come across will tell you a lot about how to manage your influence gates. For example, you'll want to open your gates to Adders and Multipliers but be more cautious around Subtractors and Dividers. You'll also want a solid trust wall to either keep the Subtractors and Dividers out of your life or simply stop them from influencing you. If you get everything else right, but your trust wall is broken down or full of holes, Subtractors and Dividers will charge into your social palace, throw out the good people, and set themselves up as the rulers of your life. Furthermore, remember that almost no one is categorically committed to being only one of these four types. People who are Adders will sometimes become afraid, insecure, or envious and act like Subtractors or even Dividers as a result. Likewise, people who are normally subtractors or dividers can *act* like Adders or Multipliers, sometimes for the sake of fulfilling a selfish intention or to find creative ways to gain the trust of others, only to sabotage at a later time. All of us have had at least one boss, employee, team member, or family member who could act as an Adder at times and a Subtractor at others.

Thus, keep in mind that humans are complicated and that the above model is nothing more than a beginner's guide. It is only by mastering the Social Capabilities below that you will build a solid defense against toxic people ***and*** attract more Adders and Multipliers into your social network. Finally, the better you can recognize these types of people, the stronger of a Social Leader you'll become.

Capability#1: Social Confidence

Social confidence starts with having definite personal standards and protecting them from negative influences both personally and professionally. This means opening the influence gates to people on your own terms instead of theirs. People with no standards or who quickly or easily compromise them, are like the proverbial city with broken walls. Confident people, on the other hand, have a solid wall around their social palace and are cautious when it comes to who they let in. I had my own revelation about the difference between deep, internal confidence, and superficial ones based on external drivers such as performance or approval of others. I've also learned through my experience that people with an internal locus of control don't feel guilty, accused, or ashamed for guarding their boundaries and sticking with their standards. That's because they are very clear about who to open up to, how soon to open up, and how much to share when they finally open up. The same principle applies to your professional interactions as well.

Like everything else, some standards are clearer than others. Therefore, some boundaries are easier to set and to stick with. For example, most people will never give a stranger the keys to their house and then leave the country for a month. That's a simple and common boundary and it's easy to recognize and enforce. What's harder to decide is when to give the keys to your soul to someone, to disclose your financial status, or to reveal your ambitions and your game plans. Most of us have fuzzy standards when it comes to these matters. Sometimes we don't have any at all. Even if we do have standards in place, we are often way too flexible with our applications. For instance, I learned early in life that entrepreneurial ambitions require clear boundaries about who to discuss those ambitions with, how soon to open up, and how much to reveal. Few will understand your desire to leave a normal job and go out on your own. Others might even be jealous of your dreams. As a result, they'll either criticize your entrepreneurial ambitions or give you unsolicited advices, usually based on little or no real experience about how to achieve your goals. Heck, some people *with* experience will still discourage you or fill your head with doubts by talking about all the obstacles *they* failed to overcome on their journey.

Therefore, it's vital to use what you've learned in the first three sections of this book to fuel your Brain, your Body, and your Spirit for maximum self-awareness, confidence, adaptability, resilience, focus, and *personal* leadership. Your mental frameworks will determine who you allow into your personal and professional circles. You'll meet people who operate mostly out of the Survival Mindset, but you'll also meet people who live in a Growth Mindset. Should you have the same set of standards for sharing information about your life and your dreams with both types? Of course not. And it will be much easier to discern and follow through with your different boundaries if you're monitoring and mastering your own mental frameworks.

The same goes for monitoring and managing your mental states and practicing the visualization techniques we discussed in the Brain Fuel section. You'll meet people whose beliefs, habits, and personal standards align with your visions. You'll also meet those whose beliefs, habits, and standards disagree or even conflict with yours. You'll meet people who help you get into your desired mental states and stay there, but you'll also come across people who try to drag you down to their level. Should you apply the same standards everywhere? Of course not. The same goes with your eating habits, exercise habits, and all other habits we talked about in the Body Fuel section. Similarly, you'll meet people who fuel their bodies with healthy foods, remain active and manage their energy well. You'll also meet people who abuse and neglect their bodies by eating junk food, keeping erratic sleep schedules, and not exercising, or skipping workouts only to waste time. Should your boundaries be the same with all these people? No, they should NOT.

Typically, we assume that confident people are simply better at attracting good relationships and leading others without noticing how they're also masters of fortifying themselves against energy vampires so they can have more room for positive and healthy relationships. People with clear personal and professional standards are attractive *because* they don't allow just anyone into their social palaces. Their standards don't even have to be that high—so long as they're clear and well-enforced. You can become one of them by practicing the Self-Leadership strategies in this book to establish high and positive personal standards and live by them. Believe me. Positive people find the quality of Self-

Leadership irresistible. So, if you're frustrated about the lack of healthy positive relationships in your life, don't worry about how you're going to start finding them. **Get clear on your own standards and start applying them to your communication.** Do this for long enough, and the people you've been trying to find will start to find you.

To start this process, begin with clarifying these three things in your personal and professional life:

WHO you'll open up to.

WHEN you'll open up to them.

HOW much you'll reveal.

By "opening up," I'm talking about sharing information about your goals, intentions, struggles, and personal hopes, fears, and passions both in your professional and personal life. If you're working on a large goal, don't start telling everyone about it. In fact, I suggest you to not bring it up at all until you've actually created some serious momentum, or until they can answer your questions and help you continue building the goal. Before you bring it into conversation, ask yourself what kind of people they are:

Are they an Adder or a Multiplier?

If they're an Adder, how might they add value to your mission? If they're a Multiplier, how might they help you multiply your outreach when you're putting your mission in action? If they're a Subtractor or a Divider, keep it to yourself even if they ask. Deflect the question and steer the conversation in another direction. Toxic people often probe with questions to pry your influence gates open. Therefore, you'd be better off keeping them shut. You are not obligated to answer a question just because someone ask. It is up to you to decide how much to share or whether to share at all. Other people can deal with their disappointments.

However, you might ask, *"Joel, what if I want to open up to someone for the sake of giving them something or influencing them in a positive way?"*

This is a good question. Of course, it's not all about you because you can't build a solid social network if you only care about yourself. But we'll talk about influencing others in a moment. For now, you must remember that if you allow someone to break down your walls, you'll have a difficult time managing your private life to even have the fuel needed to be a positive influence on others. Confidence drives Self-Leadership whereas Social-Leadership is about fortifying your social palace and conserving your energy to influence the people who deserve your time and attention. This is how you establish a strong internal locus of control and become a magnet for positive people. Once you've started working on your Social Confidence this way, you'll have additional energy for fueling the remaining four capabilities.

Capability #2: Social Adaptability

If you want to influence other people, you'll need to adapt to others' communication and negotiation styles without compromising your standards. For the same reason, it's critical for companies to adapt to technology advancements to stay relevant without changing their core values and business culture.

Compromising your standards short-circuits your ability to influence others because it tells them that you're not that serious about the things you *claim to be* important to you and you clearly don't follow through on your commitments. Meanwhile, remaining consistent with your standards will allow you to radiate social confidence and inspire trust in others.

Paul, one of Jesus' disciples and prolific Biblical author, once said that he learned to become "all things to all people" hoping he might win some to Christ. Winning people to Christ was Paul's sole mission in life and yours can be something completely different. The point is that Paul adapted to people to achieve his mission, while being someone with standards so clear and strong that he was willing to risk his life to stand by them.

How does someone have the kind of resolve that drives them to become "all things to all people?" If you've read Paul's letters in the New Testament, you'll notice how he used different figurative speaking, depending on the audience. When communicating with the Romans, he used sports and war metaphors. When speaking to people in the Asia Minor, many of whom were Gnostics, he used sayings from ancient gnostic mystery traditions. When engaging the Jewish community, he used metaphors about agriculture and referred to the Jewish law. Paul adapted his communication style based on who he was trying to influence but his message was consistent. He never wavered even when his life was in danger. Today, some historians consider Paul to be a more influential figure than Jesus Christ because of his missionary efforts to spread the word.

The same applies to our personal and professional lives today. Whether you're in a sales negotiation, on a date, or communicating with someone you've known for years, you must start by understanding their mental frameworks and communication styles. Here are a few simple questions to help you adapt to interactions with people in personal and professional settings:

Do they approach relationships with their influence gate open, closed, or locked and guarded?

This is an important question to ask especially when meeting a new person. If you get the right or a somewhat close answer, you can make significant progress in a short time. To further unpack this idea, let's look at people with open and closed gates in both personal and in professional settings.

Open Gates in Personal Settings

Be a good listener. Show empathy and bring positive, uplifting dialogues to the conversation. Empathy is one of the most common characteristics great leaders have because they know how to understand people and tap into their world even when there is a disagreement. Ask questions that will help you understand their feelings and their worldviews. Encourage laughter and light-heartedness. Don't try to give unsolicited advice. People who lead with their gates open normally just want to be heard and valued, not preached to.

Their open-hearted nature has probably allowed others to take advantages of them — maybe more than once. You can make them feel more at ease by sharing a small detail about your personal life, and asking simple, non-threatening questions about something similar in theirs. I've found that people are more likely to open up if you're willing to be transparent and authentic with them.

Open Gates in Professional Settings

Again, be a good listener. Take time to acknowledge them as an individual before getting down to business. Show empathy and look for common grounds by "listening to understand" rather than "listening to respond". Someone with closed gates might not mind your first daily communication being a business item but an open-gated person could see this as cold and impersonal. Find out what's more valuable to them and why, and look for genuine common grounds, preferably with their personal interests or hobbies. The more you take your time to connect with an open gate, the deeper your influence will be when the time arrives.

One final note on dealing with open gates is to make sure they are actually open. People with closed gates will sometimes have open communication styles and may even tell you a lot about themselves in the first meeting but remain cautious about your influence over them. Therefore, it's important to be a good listener and try to see things from their perspective before you try to influence or persuade them.

Closed Gates in Personal Settings

Assume nothing because assumptions are dangerous to begin with. Just listen and pay attention to what they're not saying. Closed-gated people often reveal more than they realize just by avoiding certain topics. Sometimes, they choose to get a feel for you before they decide to loosen up. Again, start with common grounds or ask questions while showing interest in what they're interested in. Even if their hobbies are boring to you, asking questions will help you understand *why* they're interested in these things. It will also give you an opportunity to ask them something a little more personal. If you have closed gates, you might have to open up first. Just remember your standards, go at your own pace, and don't try to push on their influence gate too soon.

Closed Gates in Professional Settings

This person might seem cold, indifferent, or even unfriendly. As a result, most people misjudge them to be rude or anti-social. Therefore, you can make a lot of progress simply by not being so quick to judge. People with closed gates are used to being misunderstood and mislabeled. Therefore, they have become accustomed to people seeing them as an enigma, a closed book, or a mystery to be solved. But deep down, everyone wants to be treated with respect. Start out by asking questions about how they are or how their day or week has been. Ask them simple questions and let their responses guide you in how or whether to proceed with the conversation at all. Don't push on their gates or assume they're closed off because they're shy or wounded. Some of the most influential leaders in history, including Gandhi, were famously quiet and unassuming around people. Most importantly, relate to their sense of humor once you get a hold of it. Humor is a great way to bond in the earlier stages without getting into personal details. Discover common interests or similarities between each other in sense of humor and move the dialogue forward into another phase. Sometimes, everything starts with simple ice-breaker questions about their hobbies or family. Do what you can to find the common ground so you can get them to open up about other things in life.

If your empathy meter tells you someone doesn't want to talk about a certain topic, trust your gut feeling and back off. Look for another approach to enter the gate. Closed-gated people are much more likely to be influenced by your actions and your competence than by your words that try to persuade them. In addition, being too aggressive with words alone might make them more suspicious of your intentions.

Finally, make sure they really are a closed-gated person. They might come off very impersonal and "strictly business" but end up being more open to your influence than you had originally thought. Others might hold back in revealing details about themselves simply for the sake of time or efficiency, or for some negotiation reason. Therefore, don't tie your hands and feet fearing that they might not be open to what you have to say. Sometimes people who seem the most closed off are eager to listen to someone who is confident and knows what they're talking about.

Asking the Right Questions

Now that we've learned a little on how to approach open and closed gates in personal and professional settings, let's review four essential questions all good leaders ask to ensure communication and positive influence.

Do they lead by talking about their personal life, professional life, or hobbies?

Sometimes you must follow before you can lead. People who talk about their personal lives in the beginning obviously want to talk about themselves, so it's best for you to relax and let them take the lead. The same goes with people who talk about their professional achievements. Instead of trying to steer them in the direction that you desire, let them talk first and then ask thoughtful questions. There's a popular myth that the person talking is the one leading the conversation, when in fact the person asking the questions is the one who is really in charge. By asking questions they're gathering information to connect themselves with the person speaking, so they can influence them later. Thus, sometimes you have to follow someone into *their* territory to be a good influencer and leader. It requires confidence to be willing to enter someone else's territory because you will be stepping out of your comfort zone. However, the more you do this, the more comfortably you can understand and communicate from someone else's perspective, instead of trying to impose yours on them.

Are they an analytical communicator or an abstract communicator?

Abstract communicators talk in stories, metaphors, and personal anecdotes. They're less responsive to facts, statistics, and long, complicated intellectual explanations. Analytical people, on the other hand, ***love*** data and science. They appreciate a well read and knowledgeable person, especially if their knowledge is on things they're interested in. Just don't try to persuade an analytical person without having a firm grasp on the facts and knowing how to apply them. Your audience will know, and you'll lose credibility quickly.

Abstract communicators also tend to have a different sense of humor than analytical people. Analytical communicators might have a cerebral or a dark sense of humor, which abstract communicators might consider weird, creepy, or stupid. Likewise, analytical communicators might think abstract communicators to be juvenile or inappropriate in their sense of humor. With some practice, you can learn to relate with both styles of humor and expand your influence on others. Take some time every week to explore diverse styles of humor by listening to different comedians than you normally would. The more effectively you can adapt your sense of humor to another communication style, the more well-rounded of a communicator and an influencer you'll become.

Do they see debates as conflicts or as opportunities to connect?

Don't underestimate the power people's perspectives on debate have. Some may enjoy a good debate and will respect you more for standing your ground and building a case for your argument. In fact, you might increase your influence with them dramatically by showing them that you're brave and articulate enough to take them on. In that case, the debate creates an opportunity to connect, build rapport, and add meaningful dialogues to your lives.

Others simply see debates as combative or a waste of time. As a result, they might mistake you for a "Divider" whether you're debating for the fun or for truly divisive reasons. You'll probably do better at persuading these people with your actions than arguments. If you let go of your "right to be right" and try to understand their perspective to resolve the conflict, these people will be much more open to your persuasions.

Thus, it's critical to understand whether someone sees a disagreement as a conflict or an opportunity to connect. Some love to match wits and feel comfortable participating in vehement debates then go have lunch together and laugh afterwards. Others walk away from disagreements furious and unwilling to talk to the other person again until they've both calmed down.

It's important to know which type of person you're talking to AND which type of person you are. If you enjoy a good debate, save your well-articulated arguments for the people who enjoy debating as much as you do. If you see debates as conflicts and you encounter someone who is up for some verbal jousting, keep your emotions in check and take them on. They'll respect you more for your courage and openness and thus see you as an equal counterpart or even a potential leader.

Are they an Adder, a Multiplier, a Subtractor, or a Divider?

This explains why you must adapt your influence gates to the person you're dealing with. If you typically lead with your gate open but get the sense that you're talking to a Subtractor or a Divider, keep your gate closed until you know for sure. People with open gates are vulnerable to divisive people, but you can avoid this trap by learning to manage your gates more diligently with Subtractors and Dividers.

Likewise, if you lead with closed gates but encounter

someone who appears to be an Adder or a Multiplier, try opening your gate a little more than usual. Just remember that Subtractors and Dividers are chameleons and masters at making good first impressions because they have no other choices as everyone would avoid them like poison. If you've ever hired someone who ended up being a total disappointment, you know what I mean. The good news is that the more you practice these techniques, the better you can discern what type of person you're talking to. At the same time, it's impossible to avoid being occasionally burned in your relationships. Sometimes, it may also be the wisest to simply avoid conflicts. This is where your third Prime Capability comes into play.

Capability #3: Social Resilience

It's reasonably easy to make a connection with someone who is like-minded and has similar communication styles. However, the best and the most rewarding connections are ones that endure through hardships and conflicts. Social resilience is vital because it allows you to turn good connections into lasting relationships. People with minimum social resilience may form temporal connections and friendships, fleeting romances, or purely transactional relationships in a professional setting. However, these connections are easily interrupted and tend to fall apart upon conflict or a mere life distraction.

Resilient people, on the other hand, enjoy consistent relationships because they know how to manage and grow them, even when the odds are against them. Think about how relationships fall apart. First, someone gets hurt. This usually happens due to a betrayal of trust. Self-preservation kicks in and the person starts to close their influence gate against the other person involved. Closed gates lead to more distrust and suspicion, and less communication. Soon, someone once close to you becomes a stranger.

However, we can avoid going down that road. Here are the three magic ingredients of mastering social resilience:

The ability to forgive.

The ability to accept forgiveness.

The capability to renegotiate trust.

People will let you down just like how you will let them down at times. No matter how much you love or respect each other, disappointments are inevitable. Therefore, the differences lay in your responses. If you want to keep the relationship, you must learn to forgive. However, this does not mean you should immediately trust them the same way you did before. People often confuse trust and forgiveness. They hold back forgiveness because they're afraid that person will hurt them, lie, or let them down again when forgiving is not the same as an immediate restoration of trust. It's the other person's job to regain your trust, especially if they genuinely did something out of line. However, they can't earn your trust back while you're secretly wanting them to suffer for what they did to you in the past.

Let's use the betrayal of a romantic partner as a relatable example. The betrayal starts when one partner cheats. The non-cheating partner finds out. A huge fight breaks, then a breakup might follow. If they decide to stay together and work it out, the partner who was cheated on often holds a grudge. In other words, they may try to repair the trust in the relationship while refusing to forgive the other person. How is this couple supposed to start restoring trust in this setting? They can't. If they want to make things work, they both have a job to do. First, the cheating partner needs to accept that their non-cheating partner may never trust them the same way they did before. If the cheating partner demands this, they are setting themselves up for a big let-down. On the other hand, the partner who was cheated on must forgive the cheating partner to start renegotiating their level of trust. This might not seem fair, since the cheating partner is the one who created the problem. But the non-cheating partner takes on this responsibility when they decide to stay in the relationship and make it work.

Finally, the offending partner must accept forgiveness and agree to negotiate trust instead of demanding it. Some people hammer themselves with guilt and shame for years after having wronged another person, even if the person they've hurt has forgiven them. This is not going to help move things forward. The right thing to do is to accept that forgiveness and be grateful while renegotiating the level of trust between the two partners. Keep in mind, again, that things won't simply snap right back to where they were before the offense was committed. Personal boundaries must be redefined along with honest and open dialogues about the progress in restoring *some* level of trust again. This is how relationships survive small conflicts as well as major ones. It goes the same when trust is violated by a business partner, boss, coworker, or employee. If you're going to keep working with or for the person, you have to renegotiate trust, and this is practically impossible if you're still secretly wanting the person to suffer for how they've wronged you.

Therefore, if you decide to keep the relationship going and make it work, you need to work with all these ingredients:

Forgiveness.

Accepting Forgiveness.

Renegotiating Trust.

Does this equation always work? Not necessarily. For the same reason, some relationships simply must end. Your relationships with Adders and Multipliers are, in most cases, worth saving. But Subtractors and Dividers often withhold forgiveness or refuse to accept it out of self-pity or the inability to heal their emotional pain. Sometimes, they'll act entitled to your trust instead of agreeing to renegotiate it. Holding onto these relationships or trying to salvage them is not a sign of social resilience. Rather, it's a sign of low self-esteem and/or unrealistic expectations about saving what can't be saved. The world is full of positive and emotionally healthy people. You deserve to enjoy personal and professional relationships that are based on love, loyalty, trust, and mutual respect. And the more you develop the social confidence and social resilience capabilities, the more you'll attract Adders and Multipliers into your life. As a result, you'll gain more energy to focus on inspiring and leading them in return.

Capability #4: Social Focus

Energy flows where you put your attention. What you focus on will manifest your reality. Therefore, if you focus your attention on people, career objectives, and social matters that bring you purpose, that's the energy you will surround yourself with. If you focus your attention on negative people, poor habits, or being lazy, that's the energy you will create and come to know. Where you put your attention, energy flows.

As we've discussed, Social Focus is also about being present and living in the moment. While the ability to "be here now" and to be a good listener has always been important, it's way more relevant today than ever, due to how technology has changed the communication paradigm. Think about it. How often do we keep our phone right next to us even if we are meeting with someone else? Being present means treating the person or the group of people you are interacting with as the most important people in the moment because you can only influence the people you're present with. In return, if you're not present, you probably won't have much influence on them.

For some of us, we remember what it was like to communicate and connect with people before social media was created. Or before cell phones became the most distractive element in social engagements. Being present was more of the norm because we weren't overly distracted and addicted to our phone and the online lives we're living. Meeting in person with people exposes you to more communication signals, including body language, facial expressions, voice tone, and—most importantly—the person's energy. That is, if we're being present and exemplifying that this current interaction in this moment matters. If we're constantly distracted with our phone face up on the table in front of us, every text, call or social media notification that comes through, drives a wedge in between the potential focused connection we could be making. There's nothing more frustrating to the individual that approaches communication with a mindset to alleviate distractions, when they're engaged in an interaction with someone that is overly distracted by their cell phone. Many people feel a sense of disrespect or immaturity toward the individual that is overly addicted and distracted by their cell phone. It ruins energy potential for the interaction and tells each member of the interaction how important they should feel around this person. Most people are understanding enough to know that there are responsibilities we all have, but be certain they're also assessing your ability to handle only the overly urgent cell phone communications within that moment. Just remember, if you want to maximize social focus, being in the present with the interactions around you is the best way to begin your practice in connecting emotionally, intellectually and spiritually. Alleviate the distractions in your control and show those around you that you value being present in your relationship with them.

So, what does it mean to practice Social Focus? It starts with intentionality. One way to do this if you need help in this arena, is keep a list of people who you want to build your *closest* relationships with. Who are the Adders and Multipliers in your life? Make it a habit of meeting with them in person as consistently as you can whether it was once a week or once a month. Keep another list of people you want to be semi-close with and meet with them in person on a consistent schedule as well, but less frequently. Also, plan what deserves your attention. This may eliminate an app that distracts you, the wrong people that interfere with your happiness and progress, or a bad habit that affects your mental health or clarity. Designing an "attention plan" can help you gain clarity on the matters that mean the most to you.

As you gain clarity on the people and matters that mean the most to you, create a framework for how you plan to lead this attention and intention.

The death bed research tells us that one of the ***top five*** regrets people have at the end of their life is losing relationships:

"I wish I had stayed in touch with my friends more.[xxxiv]*"*

What happened was that the participants didn't intentionally focus on maintaining and growing their social connections. Just like how you will need a plan to battle cravings for bad food. You need to get your body and mind in a place that resists the impulses of spending energy on things that only affect you negatively (when done excessively). In the same way, you also need an action plan if you want good, influential connections. Otherwise, you may end up with the same regret Death Bed research participants ended up with. If all this comes to you naturally, that's great. But if it doesn't, having a plan becomes that much more critical.

So, how do you start intentionally focusing on growing your relationships? You start by looking at the scientific facts about how human beings build and maintain a healthy and vibrant social network.

It is verified by experiments that you can only maintain a limited number of relationships. Keep in mind that we are not talking about LinkedIn connections, Twitter followers, or "friendships" on Facebook. Robin Dunbar, a British anthropologist, made it part of his life's work to find the "magic number" of real relationships one person can maintain.

He discovered this final number during his study of primates as there was a clear relationship between brain size and the size of sustainable social groups. He found that the neocortex, the brain's section controlling cognition and language, corresponds to the size of a primate's social network. In response, Dunbar and his colleagues applied this hypothesis to humans, using historical, anthropological, and contemporary psychological data. As a result, he found the Dunbar Number — 150.

According to Dunbar and his research team, the Dunbar Number applied to hunter-gatherer societies as well as a variety of modern settings from 11th Century English villages to modern residential campsites, communes, offices, factories, military organizations, and even Christmas card lists and wedding invitations. He also found other relevant numbers during these studies. For instance, he found that the tightest social circles consisted of five people (friends and families). He also found that people do best with 15 close friends, 50 friends, 150 contacts, 500 acquaintances, and 1500 people whom we recognize even if we can't remember their names or personal details. If you're already adequate at building and growing relationships, this hyper-mathematical approach might seem totally "out there" to you. But if building a strong professional and personal social circle doesn't come naturally, these numbers can be your guide for expanding your influence and leadership capabilities. Remember, mastering your Social Life is very similar to building a house where every single step of the process breaks down into a series of concrete action steps.

For example, start by asking yourself:

1. Who should be **your five most intimate relationships**? Plan to meet with each of them in person consistently. For example, once a week.
2. Who will **your fifteen closest friends** be? Plan to meet with each of them in person consistently. For example, once a month.
3. Who will **your fifty friends** be? Plan to connect with them multiple times a year.
4. Who will your **150 contacts** be? Create a plan to connect with them at least once a year.
5. Who will your **500 acquaintances** be? Make a plan to contact each one of them directly via text or social media consistently. For example, once a year or every few years.

You can tailor this list to your lifestyle, and you can start small. If you need help in this arena, that's a good framework to help you get started.

People who don't proactively work on their relationships are much more likely to regret it when they finally realize it's too late to do so. So, you should just do it and stay at it until these actions begin to work for you, and they will. Most importantly, when you meet with someone, be 100% present.

If someone is disgruntled because you don't answer their texts within 5 seconds, explain to them what you were doing at that point and how it will benefit them as well. If they insist on having instant, 24-7, unfiltered access to you no matter what you're doing or who you're with, that's probably someone you need to renegotiate your personal boundaries with. Remember, having and keeping standards isn't mean. Rather, it's a sign of social confidence and people of all kinds are attracted to individuals who have a personal code and live by it.

Once you start intentionally cultivating your social networks and putting your attention where it matters most, you are only one step away from becoming your most influential self.

Capability #5: Social Leadership

Social Leadership becomes much easier once you begin to work on your locus of control constantly through Self-Leadership, while intentionally cultivating your social network. Simply put, social leadership helps people discover their own voice and purpose, so you can lead a team on a common mission. Again, empathy is an essential component of social leadership. Too many aspiring leaders are more interested in imposing their will on others than understanding and helping others find their own mission on this journey. You have most likely worked for at least one leader like this. The only thing they care about is having their voice, and their voice alone, heard. But an empathetic and wise leader focuses on helping others find and express their unique voices. By "voice," I mean the intersection between their talents, passions, and their mission to use said talent and passion to impact their life.

The only thing rarer than talent is the ability to recognize someone else's talent and use different talents from different individuals toward a common goal together. That's the essence of leadership. The leader is the captain of an organization's culture, whether it is a company, a team, or a family. Great leaders know how to create a victory-driven environment by holding people accountable, providing continuous visions and a culture for winning, while creating continued progress. In this environment team members should feel comfortable expressing their ideas while pointing out problems within the organization safely and freely.

However, Social Leadership goes beyond leading a team or organization toward a common goal. A good leader inspires someone to find their voice and their life's direction even if that person heads toward a different horizon in the end. Leaders know when to follow, when to listen and when to make bold decisions for a team for its safety and prosperity. Their care for the team is sensed and felt.

But people want to follow winners. People want to follow individuals they feel are stronger than themselves, while also not feeling like their growth and success will be held back or hindered in the environment. Your ability to create this culture of winning, growth and individual impact, creates a team force and energy similar to the synergy we discussed earlier in the chapter. 1+1=3 and the best leaders find ways to get 1+1+1+1 to equal far more than those numbers added together. Leader's ability to get the right individuals in the right seat in an organization or group, while entrusting their voice to be heard and team communications synergized, is a superpower of the best. Whether in an organization or a social group, these components and personal attributes hold true.

It all begins with your ability to manage your own self-leadership. Developing your personal capabilities will directly develop your social leadership ability and help you transcend your leadership capability gap.

As you continue on your social leadership journey, understand the power of influence, how it works and how leaders impact in many different ways. It's not always be being a great direct leader in an organization or group. In fact, you'll become a leader among your social networks simply by:

1. Pursuing your life's mission

2. Inspiring others to find their *mission*

3. Becoming a social connector

The first step is self-explanatory. People who know where they're going are much more likely to become leaders because all they need is the right connections and the four social capabilities. Because their locus of control is already internal, it makes them immune to negative influences. Meanwhile, people who don't know where they're going or simply aren't consistently pursuing their goals can't lead anyone for long, even if they have an amazing social network. I can't overstate how important it is that you build up some momentum in your private life first before heading into the social leadership realm.

Once you've started creating positive momentum in your private life, a next step is learning the power of being a Social Connector. I encouraged you to make a plan to grow your social connections by progressing from your five most intimate relationships to your fifteen closest friends, your fifty regular friends, your pool of 150 contacts, and eventually, your wider network of acquaintances. Then, we can talk about becoming what author Malcolm Gladwell calls a "connector." Simply put, a connector is someone who, intentionally or habitually, has built such a strong network of relationships that they become the hub through which people connect with one another, form new personal relationships, and secure new professional alliances.

Imagine if married couples, business partners, friends, and other social connections came into connection because of this power you built. This is what a connector does. You don't have to be a social butterfly to become a connector, either. You don't even have to build a massive social network. The only thing you need is the intention to become someone who connects people especially if you're not naturally inclined to meeting new people or building connections. Again, it's all about being proactive. If building your social circle already comes naturally to you and you just need some motivation, great. Go do it! Otherwise, just keep in mind that everything can be broken down into a set of logical steps and turned into a natural habit. Let's revisit Dunbar's Numbers for a plan on how you can do this

1. Who are **your five most intimate relationships?**
2. Who are **your fifteen closest friends?**
3. Who are **your fifty regular friends?**
4. Who are your **150 contacts?**
5. Who are your **500 acquaintances?**

Who else in your social network can you introduce these people to? What kind of social gathering could YOU create to make these connections possible?

Don't worry. I'm not asking you to throw weekly block parties or run around introducing people to one another. You can naturally become a connector at your own pace. Be patient with this, just be aware that it's a great way to help connections of yours out without expecting anything in return. Your influence will be felt and appreciated. Just make sure you're connecting the right people or it can be the wrong influence you're creating. That's why it's important to be patient and strategic with this approach.

By performing this skill effectively you're expressing your social leadership ability. This will also lead to more positive energy that you create all around you.

Besides becoming a connector, suppose you have an intentional mission in life and you are consistently fueling your Brain, Body, and Spirit, then, it is only a matter of time for people to be drawn to you and your social network. In return, doors will open in places where there seems to be nothing but walls right now. This is the power of navigating from Self-Leadership to Social Leadership. The fuel and momentum that Social Leadership creates for your life is ***unmatched***.

From Social Leadership to Social Legacy

You now have the knowledge to make this next decade the

best decade of your life. What will you do with it? If you're unsure about where to start, don't worry. I'll guide you in our final section. But before we move on, there is one final aspect about Social Fuel we must cover.

While sometimes you need to be around others, other times you may need to be alone to practice Self-Leadership. Finding this balance is a major part of making the skills and knowledge covered in this book work in your favor. Isolating yourself from quality social institutions can be the most detrimental component for your communication skills, building and maintaining quality relationships and the social fuel you need to level up. Therefore, learning how to balance your private time with your social time is vital.

Nonetheless, that balance is different for everyone. As an extrovert, I found it difficult to separate myself from the world to write and work on independent projects for large blocks of time. I didn't find much joy being alone at the beginning. However, solitude is probably a lot more comfortable for a stark introvert than it is for someone like me. This doesn't make introverts *or* extroverts more or less equipped to master any of the Five Prime Capabilities. It simply shows why each category should consider an approach that matches their personality type.

For example, the more I am in solitude, the more I've come to enjoy it. But I've also had no problem maintaining my connections with those who matter most. If you're an introvert, your ability to process thought and enter creative thinking can become slightly addicting. But too much time alone can turn solitude into isolation, which cuts us off from vital human interactions. Again, it's a delicate balance and everyone must find their own rhythm. The more I'm able to enjoy being alone to create, reflect, and think, the more I appreciated the power of healthy intimate relationships. In other words, my time alone has allowed me to build stronger relationships when I do spend time around people.

Of course, it's better being alone than being around people who bring you down. The more you develop your life, the more tempting privacy and solitude may become —I feel this even as an extrovert.

"What will people say about you after you're gone?"

Will they care? What impact will you have?

CHAPTER 8:
THE ENTOURAGE EFFECT

COMBINING FORCES TO UNLEASH YOUR MOST CAPABLE SELF

"You don't have to be great to start, but if you want to be great, you have to start."

-Zig Ziglar

Do you feel stuck? Stuck in a role that's stealing all motivation and energy necessary to create forward movement?

Are you struggling to develop momentum for an area in your life that's important for your fulfillment or progress?

Do you have poor habits that have been destructive to the path you feel destined to be on?

Is your performance inconsistent or lacking in an area of your life that is bringing you disappointment or anxiety? Is it affecting your ability to get quality sleep?

Have you stepped into a new arena and are seeking the capabilities and fuels necessary for leveling up to activate ideal momentum?

We are all on different journeys and will need different formulas to fuel our most capable self. We each have different circumstances, genetics, health goals, and destinations we desire, but many of principles and practices we discussed throughout this book are universal in obtaining abundance in our lives. Depending on what journey you are on, will also depend on which capabilities are most important for you to focus on to generate the momentum and leading you closer to capturing your most capable self. Regardless, your ability to fuel your Five Prime Capabilities and get them working to an optimal level, while using the momentum you generate as your additional power source, will tell a story about the life you lead. This is the power of the Entourage Effect working in your life.

The Entourage Effect is getting your Prime Capabilities working together by fueling your most abundant Brain, Body, Spirit and Social Capability Fuels. When you can collectively combine these forces consistently, your ability to create positive momentum for your Self and Social Leadership journey will be maximized. Your ability to create more of your best days will be in full force and those around you will feel your energy and power.

And no, when we speak of the Entourage Effect, we are not discussing the drama series, Entourage, featuring Vince and his clan, although there's some relatable elements to the social camaraderie that fuels a group's performance. We are also not discussing the CBD and cannabinoid Entourage Effect, when these elements work together for a balanced psychoactive effect. What we ***are*** talking about, is when you get these capabilities and fuels working together to help you unleash your most capable self. Your most capable self that can step into any arena, adapt quickly, and perform at an optimal level with confidence and influence. As you get the Entourage Effect working for you in its most dynamic form, you'll feel its existence and you'll hopefully maintain your discipline, to sustain its power.

Hopefully you've been able to gain a few pieces of knowledge throughout this book to help you on your journey forward to generating the momentum you desire and for developing your most capable self. Take a moment if you haven't already to break down exactly what information you need to implement into your life consistently, with discipline, over the next 6 months. Then, do your best to narrow this objective down into 1 precise sentence or activity you want to start with. The more precise you can pinpoint exactly what you're trying to accomplish, the more clarity you'll have as you introduce it repeatedly into your life.

Remember, for many of these momentum gains, they're more complex than just making a small change. Most individuals that strive for improved performance in one area of their life, find themselves working on multiple components to activate and maximize the momentum. For example, if you want to increase your performance by getting better, intentional sleep, there's multiple components that play a factor here. If you choose to eat healthier but aren't getting proper exercise, creating a good sleep routine or are consuming too many of the wrong substances, you may not see a large impact. In addition, if you're going to bed looking at your cell phone or your mind is spinning on too many thoughts that are stressing you out, your sleep quality will suffer.

So as you pinpoint exactly what your goal is, work to break down the goal to understanding all the components necessary to increase its likeliness and proficiency. The more you are able to get these components, fuels and capabilities working together, the more you'll have the power to level up and perform as your most capable self.

As you work to fuel and develop these capabilities, make sure you're not hijacked by a leak in your tank. Leaks are small to large cracks that deplete our energy source and hold us back from optimizing our willpower. If there's an area in your life that needs attention or an alternate fuel source, work on this first. I realize change isn't easy and I can relate to how just "fixing a leak" isn't always that easy. BUT, with intentional focus and disciplinary action daily, I'm confident you'll repair the leak and can start to generate the momentum that you desire. No one is coming to save you, but yourself (when you commit to that choice). You are in charge of saving you. YOU are in charge of the leveling up necessary to activate the desired momentum. The mini-discipline adjustments you're about to make is the force you need to transcend your capability gaps and get your momentum moving forward with optimal progress.

Fuel Your Choices

Anytime you try to activate new momentum on a new venture, the initial momentum is always the most difficult. Going from 0-1 is much harder than going from 1-5 on your journey. That's because making the decision to navigate on a new journey has a lot of friction working against you. Whether it's the knowledge and skill necessary to be effective, the new habits you're effortlessly disciplining into your life or unknown elements that meet you along the way. They will be there and you'll have to adjust and level up. But, once you're able to activate and generate some momentum by integrating consistently, you'll be able to use this momentum to maximize your efficiency toward your destination.

If you get discouraged or lose motivation early on, in any way, you now have another force working against you, yourself. But, if you stay the course and proceed with grit and determination, you'll make it off the starting line from 0-1 and then you can use that momentum and the collective efforts of your capabilities you're developing, to move from 1-5, generating additional momentum.

Once you generate momentum, it's like getting a boulder rolling downhill. Inertia has already begun and it's working for you, with you. Unfortunately, sometimes activating this momentum, takes pushing this boulder up the hill for four to twelve months, first. Momentum and energy are funny like this, but once they're on your side, it's a beautiful manifestation. If you've ever had it and lost it, you know what I'm talking about.

To help you move this boulder up the hill and activate the desired levels of momentum toward your most capable self, I've developed a four-stage practice to help you fuel your Five Prime Capabilities most effectively. Building habits and routines with these new approaches is the link to making these fuels work for you most optimally.

This four-stage practice is based on the general stages we experience when we turn a new piece of knowledge into action so it can eventually develop into a habit that benefits you the rest of your life.

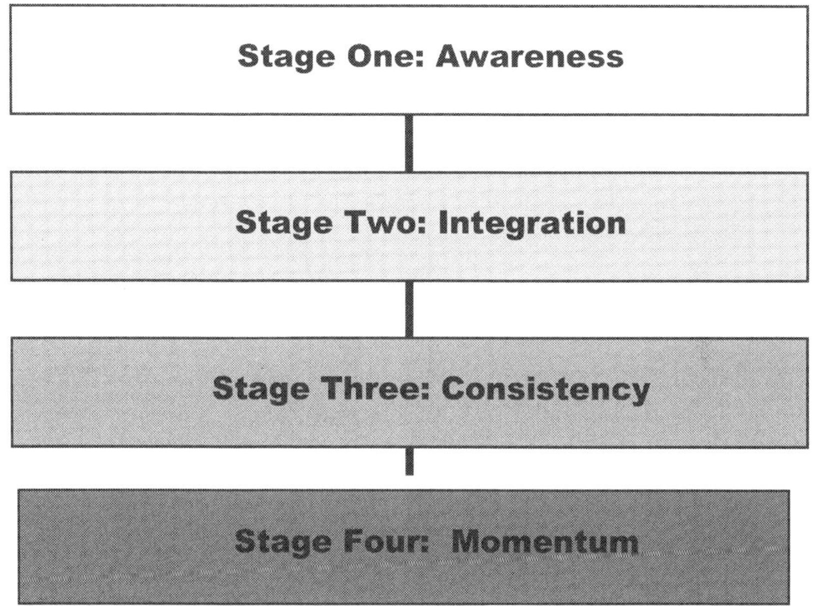

Stage One: Awareness

The secret to the awareness stage is to choose one solid piece of information from this book and make that the prime focus of your attention, until it saturates your consciousness. Start with one piece of knowledge because overwhelming yourself with multiple inputs will diminish your focus power and make the integration and consistency stages much harder.

By focusing on one piece of knowledge and soaking it into your awareness over the next several days and weeks, you will begin to rewire your brain through the neuroplasticity principles we've discussed earlier. So, go back to the Brain Fuel, Body Fuel, Spirit Fuel *or* Social Fuel section and find that one nugget of knowledge you'd like to begin with and make sure what you choose is consistent with your Primary Intention. For example, if you were attracted to the section about how to develop a Growth Mindset, start there by turning that knowledge into a simple daily action. Alternatively, suppose you found something that really caught your eyes in the Body Fuel section, choose one idea that you can start to practice immediately. The point is, you should find a simple and singular focus, so you give yourself the chance to build up some momentum before new things start piling up on you.

Also, make sure to choose something you ***know*** will be extremely impactful to your life and don't worry about anything else until you've got this idea deeply seeded in your mind. Write your choice down once you've made up your mind and place it somewhere you can it see throughout the day. You might want to write it on a notecard and place it somewhere you see it every morning or turn it into an image and set it as the screensaver on your phone or laptop. Again, make sure you pick one piece of knowledge from this book and place this goal somewhere you can see it each day.

If you're feeling super ambitious, feel free to use the visualization practice from the Brain Fuel section to get this idea embedded into your consciousness more thoroughly. At some point, the idea will saturate your awareness that you can't stop thinking about it. That's when you're ready to move forward.

Stage Two: Integration

Now that you have saturated your awareness with your chosen piece of knowledge, it's time to integrate your awareness with your daily actions by creating a simple action that you can easily repeat every day. For example, if you spent Stage One focusing on the idea of developing a Growth Mindset, you may want to set aside ten minutes every day to develop that mindset further. Whenever you find yourself in a reactive, survival, or fixed mindset, note your response and how you could reframe that thought pattern into a growth-focused one. Take that new idea and focus on it during visualization or meditation practices. You can visualize a positive conversation with your spouse or a coworker after noticing yourself getting into an argument with the person. That way, you practice to talk and to listen out of a Growth Based Mindset.

Alternatively, you might set aside ten minutes in the evening to write in a journal about what mindset you had during the day. Did you maintain a Growth Mindset? Or did you act out of a Survival Mindset? Finally, why did you behave or think the way you did? How can you make a different choice tomorrow? What choice would that be?

No matter what the goal is, the key here is to choose a repeatable action so it can develop into a consistent habit with daily reinforcements. Don't get too relaxed during this stage. Instead, focus on your daily action, keep your attention intense, and stay highly alert. Intensive focus will stimulate the appropriate release of adrenaline, acetylcholine, and other excitatory neurotransmitters that instruct your brain to direct its neuroplasticity efforts toward the new habit you're working on.

When done right, you will clearly feel your physiological state change as you develop your habit. If you don't feel this change right away, that's fine. Keep grinding every day and eventually you will see the differences. As the new habit becomes second nature, this changed state also begins to relax. This process creates muscle memory subconsciously and overtime it will take less energy to perform it consistently.

Once that happens, it's time for you to find new ways to maintain that intensive focus on the task so you continue to release those excitatory neurotransmitters and promote neuroplasticity. In other words, you should not be completely relaxed when working on your daily action. Instead, you should maintain an intensive focus that it almost makes you uncomfortable. That's because a completely relaxed state cannot promote neuroplasticity. Thus, it will eventually lead to complacency. However, if you can balance focus and relaxation, you'll encourage neuroplasticity during your practice and your brain will continue to rewire itself even when you are resting.

So as you navigate integrating your mini-discipline adjustments into your life to level up, remember it's not supposed to be easy, and discomfort is expected.

Stage Three: Consistency

Consistency can be the simplest stage. However, it's also the stage where goals are lost and where most people quit because they fail to commit to the change, the pain of leveling up or lose focus or motivation along the way. Up till now, it's about putting in the work to find a piece of knowledge to focus on. From here on, it requires the right strategy, commitment, and motivations so you can stay in that state of mind and continue to grow.

Being consistent is rather self-explanatory but tends to be the most difficult for people. Our bodies naturally do almost anything to put you into a relaxed and comfortable setting. When you step into these new routines, your body and mind initiate survival instincts and many people allow these instincts to have too much power. This is why change and consistency can be difficult. I never said it was going to be easy. In fact, it will be very painful and difficult at times. But, I'm confident you'll make the decision to push past the discomfort and find your groove with consistency.

Consistent actions crystalize into habits and your habits shape your life. Be consistent daily, momentum will follow and you're that much closer to your most capable self.

Stage Four: Momentum

By the time you reach this stage, you should have spent three to twelve months working on the first three stages. In a world where everyone wants instant gratification, real momentum takes time and consistency. You should *feel* the cumulative momentum starting to fuel your confidence, adaptability, resilience, focus, and leadership capabilities. This is the Entourage Effect. It's getting your fuels and capabilities working for you and together to create an energy force forward, that generates ideal momentum. As you get these capabilities fueled effectively and activate momentum, the momentum becomes an additional energy source, fueling back into your capabilities and the momentum that it can produce. When the Entourage Effect is in full force, your Master Capability of Momentum becomes your additional energy source that has the ability to create dream like success, fulfillment and Social Leadership opportunities.

To circle back to your Primary Intention you first established while reading this book, how has this intention changed in complexity? Have you discovered a few integrations necessary to create momentum for this intention?

If your Primary Intention is big enough to scare you as much as it excites you, you're on the right track. The trick is to push yourself hard enough to shock your brain back into neuroplasticity mode by releasing those excitatory neurotransmitters. Large intentions take larger intentional leveling up.

If you're feeling stuck or you're trying to access momentum on a new journey, remember Newton's First Law of Motion, where a body at rest stays at rest while a body in motion tends to stay in motion. The same goes for being stuck and becoming unstoppable. Once you've activated your momentum, you are most likely to keep moving forward, as long as your focus and actions stay consistent.

From Momentum to Mastery

Mastery is the ability to recycle the momentum to fuel itself. It's your ability to use the Entourage Effect to its full effect.

Remember, a Capability is an intrinsic characteristic which expands your ability to perform a specific skill or set of skills.

In return, it increases your likelihood of continual progression toward your goals. This expansion only happens through the maximization and refinement of your Prime

Capabilities using the brain, body, spirit, and social fuels.

Applying this four-stage practice will increase the probability of you making the movement in life you desire and helping you achieve your Primary Intention. This energy will fuel you to integrate more positive actions to create more momentum. Eventually, it catapults you to new levels of growth. When done correctly, you'll realize why Momentum is the Master Capability. It is the gateway into mastery, which is another powerful Capability Fuel that exponentially increases your potential for achieving things beyond your original intention.

Progress is another type of fuel as it leads you into new territories, expands your awareness, and provides fuel for your confidence, from the actions you've been taking daily. If you're not taking disciplinary action and therefore not making progress, your confidence can be greatly impacted. Once again, you can't fool your mind into believing you're confident when your actions tell you a different story. Therefore, your ability to be disciplined and make progress, fuels your first Prime Capability, confidence, which is the skeleton key for all your Prime Capabilities.

Each milestone large or small that you reach offers a release of dopamine, the feel-good chemical. Progress can fuel you to generate chemical motivation. If you focus on this progress each day, the chemical momentum can turn into that extra daily fuel we need sometimes, to keep pushing forward and leveling up our capabilities daily.

As you continue to develop these capabilities and generate momentum;

You'll adapt quickly to new opportunities and overcome unexpected obstacles with astounding energy and confidence.

You'll become more resilient in the face of adversity and you will use failures as stepping-stones toward your next desired outcome.

Your focus will become so intense that you'll only see objectives to accomplish. The obstacles and distractions which once towered over you like mountains, will now look like measly anthills that are one action away from overcoming.

Most importantly, this newfound Self-Leadership will develop into Social Leadership as you become a generator of positive influence to everyone you meet.

However, everything starts with small daily actions. Mini-discipline adjustments that are filled with friction, but eventually create progress. Thus, this chapter will serve as your gateway into making all the knowledge in this book ***work for you***.

"Discipline will take you places motivation can't" – Bill Masur

You have the ability to break past the mental and physical limitations that have held you back for years and into a life where anything is possible. A life of possibilities, all within your control. This can be your life from now on. All you need to do is create a plan, START and commit to pushing this boulder up the hill, with **consistent daily action**.

Positive Momentum is in your future.

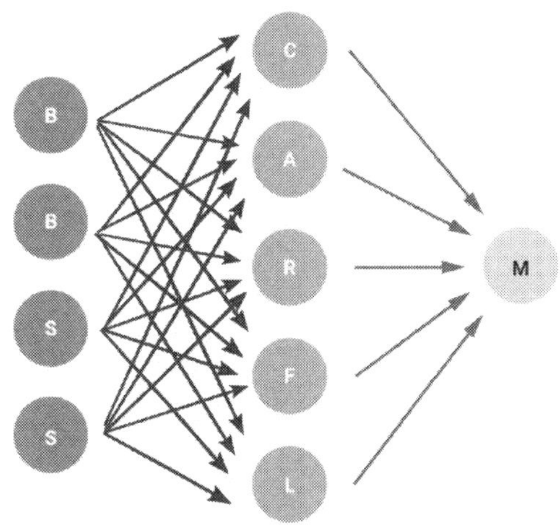

B = Brain Fuel
B = Body Fuel
S = Spirit Fuel
S = Social Fuel

C = Confidence
A = Adaptability
R = Resilience
F = Focus
L = Leadership

M = Momentum

Momentum

Confidence
Adaptability
Resilience
Focus
Leadership

Brain Fuel
Body Fuel
Spirit Fuel
Social Fuel

About the Author

THE BEGINNING

I grew up in a large family, one of eight kids, where every child constantly competed against one another in just about everything. The desire to win, therefore, always motivated and inspired me to understand strategy and to develop specific capabilities in everything I did, to maximize my performance.

When I made my way to college to play baseball, I pushed myself to win out different starting positions I desired to play, to help my team win and maximize the challenge. I went from right field, to center, to shortstop and closing pitcher. If I could develop an added skill to my performance arsenal, I always learned ways to increase my determination and work ethic to accomplish it. I also had to pay my way through school, in what I didn't receive from scholarships. While going to school and playing baseball, I also learned to run a small business to pay my way through school. Work ethic and discipline were always on my side.

As I continued to grow up and enter my career of business consulting, strategy continued to fascinate me. By the time I was 25, I began reading every business, personal development and financial book I could get my hands on. I wanted to maximize my ability to perform, while also helping the young entrepreneurs and clients I was working with, do the same. I also wanted to be able to activate the characteristics I gained through physical training, mental practices, and through my leadership experience on cue. I wanted to build my confidence and adaptability to be able to handle any challenge, event, or performance at my highest potential. In reality, I just wanted to win, all of the time. Even to a default at times. I wanted to progress my life in its most successful and fulfilled form. Of which was business, travel, relationships and life experiences.

As I worked with young entrepreneurs and sales professionals in my 20s, I also found a home in Charlotte, NC. As I navigated building my consulting career in my mid-20s, I developed a program designed to help young adults build successful small businesses, while helping them overcome the chaos and obstacles on this journey. It became a huge passion of mine to understand one's capabilities as they pursue individually designed journeys toward achieving specific goals. As enriching as the journey and the people that I've met along the way have been, there has also been some extremely difficult experiences that impacted my way of understanding this life and the fuels that empower, deplete and move us through our unique path.

LIFE'S FUEL COMPLEXITIES

Frankly, I wasn't prepared for the next cluster of events in my life. Up until that point, nothing overly severe had entered my life. No shockwave events had impacted me to the point of questioning my existence to its foundational reality. My lifestyle and philosophy were mostly self-focused with an emphasis on winning in each area of my development.

Then, I lost Zac, my cousin and great friend, in a tragic accident. Zac was an incredible athlete and a source of tremendous positive energy.

Losing Zac was devastating for the whole family because he was one of those guys everyone gravitated toward. Everyone was attracted to his contagious characteristics and the spirit he embodied. But for me, it was more than that. We'd always sought each other out when we competed against our fellow cousins at our large family events. He was usually the best teammate anyone could have for winning and maximizing fun.

Unfortunately for me and all the people Zac had in his influence circle, we lost Zac, only 25 years of age, to a tragic accident that sent a shockwave throughout our family.

I'd do anything to be on the same team with Zac one more time. Suddenly, I realized how fragile life could be. How you could lose someone at any given time. You would leave so much unsaid and undone.

After Zac's tragedy, I poured my heart into my team and business to create as much success and impact as possible.

Just 10 months later, the next tragic event occurred.

Every year, I took my top performers on a cruise to the Bahamas for a three-day mini-vacation to celebrate their achievements that year. The group would be anywhere from forty to sixty people. They came from different parts of the country.

Eventually, my people became a second family. I was there when they navigated through the highs and lows of managing their first business. Many of us were our strongest relationships to one another.

On the last evening of a cruise in 2014, a few of them decided to climb to a spot on the ship for the best view of the sunrise over Miami as we neared the coast to dock early in the morning. Around 5:00 am, I got a call to my cabin informing me that one of my young inspirations, Kendall, had fallen and was in critical condition.

As the ship made an emergency docking, I jumped into the front seat of the ambulance, shaking, my heart filled with prayers. I still remember the panic I had and my fury toward the vehicles in the streets as the driver navigated heavy Miami traffic that morning. The thirty minutes in the emergency room felt like an eternity as I sat there waiting for what I hoped would be a recovery story. *This can't happen. Not to him, not now. He has so much to accomplish still. God, he is too young. He has too much to offer the world. Please. Save him. Spare him. Spare all of us. Please.*

Eventually, a hospital manager greeted me and sat me down.

"Give me good news," I said. "Please."

"This is not the news today, I'm sorry Mr. Puthoff. We could not save him."

No words could possibly describe the emotions that swept through my body. I was his leader and felt a level of responsibility for protecting him. A young man with such a compassionate heart and a beautiful mind was taken from all of us. He had so much good to offer this world and none of that should be stripped away so early. It still breaks my heart today recalling the phone call I made to his parents when the ship tried to make an emergency docking, telling them their son had fallen and was fighting for his life. Breaking this news to his family and our entire team that loved this kid so much was remarkably gut-wrenching.

I failed to protect my people.

I boarded my plane home as an empty shell of who I was the evening before. I can still feel the weight of his suitcase in my hand as endless tears soiled my shirt on my trip home. It felt like losing a little brother.

What I didn't expect was how everything I knew about this amazing young man over the past few years became more understood as I spent some difficult hours and days with his family. I will never forget his family's ability to handle the situation. I was humbled and astonished by their strength and compassion in such a dire moment. It was unlike anything I'd ever witnessed. I realized that Kendall showed the influence his family had on him in so many ways.

A few days later, I stood before hundreds of people to give a part of his eulogy. All I wanted was to give others a small piece of what this young man had given all of us. The impact he had on our entire team and those connected to us. At the end, I asked everyone impacted by this young man's life to stand up. One by one, the entire congregation rose to their feet. A slow ripple of love and gratitude swelled from the center of that congregation as everyone in the church was on their feet, showing their support for the family. That feeling in that moment is far deeper than any emotion I have ever been in contact with in my life.

The energy in the church that day created an entire new level of energy existence in my world. I'm not sure I will ever be connected to such a deep and profound energy source, filled with love, heartbreak, confusion, and overall connectedness to such a large group. I realized the narrow and categorical ambitions we embrace are nothing but finite representations of this power as it seeks expression through us. It lives and exists in each one of us.

Since then, I made it my mission to introduce this energy into the relationships in my life and use it to fuel my ambitions for this short time we're all fortunate enough to have.

Losing both Zac and Kendall were very difficult and their memories will certainly be with me for the rest of my time here on earth. But there's also many other complexities to the fuels that have influenced my actions and behaviors. I've had ups and downs with my business journeys, I've been in and out of love that crushed and confused me, I've found myself questioning my path or having doubts throughout my journeys, feeling stuck or confused about the next move, triumphant in victory, discouraged in another championship loss, and have experienced the rush or climbing mountains, leading teams and inspiring others to do similar.

Learning how to manage the ebbs and flows of uncertainty, doubt, excitement, passion, victory, defeat, disappointment, and all other emotionally present chemicals, while maintaining clarity and confidence along the way, is one beautiful journey we all get to experience. It just doesn't always feel so beautiful. It can twist and turn into dark and confusing times, especially when you feel your choices could have been sharper throughout the journey. Yes, we all make mistakes and that's the beauty of free will and individual pursuits we lead.

All these experiences led me on a journey that pushed me to crank my studying and learning dial up to its highest mark. Along the way I gathered an intense understanding of these fuel complexities, while also learning how to manage them most effectively. As I was working on a new business journey and still trying to compete in competitive sports, I buried my mind into human science books, looking to gain new knowledge for prolonging my physical performance, increasing my mental capacity and extending my spiritual and social well-being. There were many things I was learning, but not yet practicing, and I yearned to understand the extent of my capabilities for this one life.

How could I understand myself and this world well enough to build a roadmap for this one journey I get to experience? Full of intention. With an understanding that it can end at any time.

I began to look deeper into what transcended each aspect of human performance — the fuels and how they work together to propel human development.

At the beginning, I focused on the internal fuels we supply ourselves while understanding the negative influences that present themselves to disrupt our capability development.

Soon after, I developed an intense curiosity regarding how to maximize human capability fuels scientifically, and with a customized habit routine.

While I have always been physically fit, I had not yet approached my journey with using my learnings and habits to "fuel my most abundant self." Each new journey for me, required a different manual for success and now my habits needed to shift again for my new journey of mental performance and the new startup venture I was pursuing.

I knew I needed to improve my routines, starting with my diet, my thought processes, how I spent my free time and my plan for long-term health and wellness. This also triggered my motivation to become a better learner, writer and communicator. From that point on, I began to learn how to FUEL my most transcendent capabilities.

While I continued working with entrepreneurs, I spent more time discovering how other entrepreneurs, business leaders and high performers with a desire to level up, approached similar challenges. But there was no single book that covered all the fuels needed for abundancy in life, personal health, and achievement. As I learned from so many other high performers the power of writing, I stepped up my journaling intensity and began writing about all the knowledge I gathered from highly credible sources and from my experiences daily. My writing goals took a bold leap when I set out to create a holistic, refined source for understanding the FUELS that propel our most capable self.

DEDICATION

I'd like to dedicate this book to Zac Richard and Kendall Wernet, of which both individuals inspired me to fulfill my life with the utmost intention. Your character and zest for life will never be forgotten.

ENDNOTES

[i] https://www.forbes.com/sites/brentgleeson/2019/03/06/what-navy-seals-can-teach-us-about-adaptability/#4cff95cd4b6e

[ii] https://www.forbes.com/sites/jeffboss/2016/04/26/staying-competitive-requires-adaptability/#f66d1b47e6f9

[iii] https://www.youtube.com/watch?v=jYcnaYEzX7Y

[iv] https://www.liveabout.com/george-foreman-career-record-424252

[i] https://www.britannica.com/science/information-theory/Physiology

[vi] http://news.mit.edu/2017/brain-waves-reflect-different-types-learning-1011

[vii] https://chriskresser.com/sympathetic-vs-parasympathetic-state-how-stress-affects-your-health/

[viii] https://www.simplypsychology.org/cognitive-dissonance.html

[ix] https://www.ncbi.nlm.nih.gov/pmc/articles/PMC4417372/

[x] https://www.chicagotribune.com/opinion/ct-xpm-2010-08-10-ct-oped-0811-multitask-20100810-story.html

[xi] https://www.apa.org/monitor/may02/useit

[xii] https://www.webmd.com/lung/coronavirus

[xiii] https://www.urologyofva.net/articles/category/healthy-living/3531968/what-is-inflammation

[xiv] https://www.integrativepsychiatry.net/brain_inflammation.html

[xv] https://chriskresser.com/how-to-optimize-your-brain-for-better-cognitive-performance/

[xvi] https://www.ncbi.nlm.nih.gov/pmc/articles/PMC4396848/

[xvii] https://medical-dictionary.thefreedictionary.com/acquired+reflex

[xviii] https://www.youtube.com/watch?v=XpaOjMXyJGk

[xix] http://theleadsouthaustralia.com.au/industries/health-and-medical/study-finds-best-exercise-to-stretch-your-brain/

[xx] https://www.cbc.ca/news/health/food-cravings-engineered-by-industry-1.1395225

[xxi] https://406acupuncture.com/10-fake-names-for-high-fructose-corn-syrup/

[xxii] https://www.health.harvard.edu/blog/nutritional-psychiatry-your-brain-on-food-201511168626

[xxiii] https://www.orthoatlanta.com/media/the-correlation-between-dehydration-and-orthopedic-injuries#:~:text=It's%20recommended%20that%20you%20stay,injuries%2C%20such%20as%20orthopedic%20injuries.

[xxiv] https://www.ncbi.nlm.nih.gov/pubmed/22848760

[xxv] https://ghr.nlm.nih.gov/gene/BDNF

[xxvi] https://www.coachmag.co.uk/lifestyle/4511/ectomorph-endomorph-or-mesomorph-what-is-your-body-type

[xxvii] https://www.heart.org/en/healthy-living/fitness/fitness-basics/aha-recs-for-physical-activity-in-adults

[xxviii] https://neurohacker.com/anti-aging-benefits-of-intermittent-fasting

[xxix]

https://www.theguardian.com/lifeandstyle/2016/nov/28/breakfast-health-america-kellog-food-lifestyle

[xxx] https://www.psychologytoday.com/us/blog/do-the-right-thing/201102/could-lower-expectations-result-in-happier-life

[xxxi] https://www.ncbi.nlm.nih.gov/pmc/articles/PMC2944261/

[xxxii] https://www.psychalive.org/dr-daniel-siegel-neuroplasticity/

[xxxiii] https://time.com/5373403/surprising-benefits-introvert/

[xxxiv] https://insight.kellogg.northwestern.edu/article/how-to-maintain-strong-friendships-as-you-move-through-your-career

MTG,

The Ohio superstar turned Charlotte entrepreneur!

I appreciate the friendship we've grown over the years. We survived Covid together and I love the diversity of dialogue we've shared.

To all our future endeavors we have the opportunity to experience! I look forward to them.

May The Force Be With You!

Joel Bernard

Made in the USA
Columbia, SC
01 April 2021